W9-CQM-919

LIBRETTO/VOCAL BOOK

HAROLD PRINCE
presents

Fiddler on the Roof

Book by **JOSEPH STEIN**
(based on Sholem Aleichem's stories by special permission of Arnold Perl)

Lyrics by **SHELDON HARNICK**   Music by **JERRY BOCK**

Entire Production Directed & Choreographed by
JEROME ROBBINS

NOTICE: **DO NOT DEFACE!**

Should you find it necessary to mark cues or cuts, use a **SOFT BLACK LEAD PENCIL ONLY.**

**NOT FOR SALE.
FOR PROFESSIONAL USE ONLY.**

This book is rented and remains the property of:

MUSIC THEATRE INTERNATIONAL
545 Eighth Avenue
New York, NY 10018

(212) 868-6668

CAST OF CHARACTERS
(In Order of Appearance)

TEVYE, the Dairyman
GOLDE, his wife
TZEITEL, HODEL, CHAVA, SHPRINTZE, BIELKE, his daughters
YENTE, the Matchmaker
MOTEL, the Tailor
PERCHIK, the Student
LAZAR WOLF, the Butcher
MORDCHA, the Innkeeper
RABBI
MENDEL, his Son
AVRAHM, the Bookseller
NACHUM, the Begger
GRANMA TZEITEL
FRUMA-SARAH
CONSTABLE
FYEDKA
SHAINDEL, Motel's Mother
THE FIDDLER
VILLAGERS

SCENES

THE PLACE: ANATEVKA, A SMALL VILLAGE IN RUSSIA
THE TIME: 1905, ON THE EVE OF THE RUSSIAN
               REVOLUTIONARY PERIOD

ACT ONE

ACT TWO

Prologue

TEVYE

A fiddler on the roof. Sounds crazy, no? But in our little
village of Anatevka, you might say every one of us is a
fiddler on the roof, trying to scratch out a pleasant,
simple tune without breaking his neck. It isn't easy. You
may ask, why do we stay up there if it's so dangerous? We
stay because Anatevka is our home. ... And how do we keep
our balance? That I can tell you in a word . . Tradition.

CHORUS

TRADITION, TRADITION ... TRADITION
TRADITION, TRADITION ... TRADITION

TEVYE

Because of our traditions, we've kept our balance for many,
many years. Here in Anatevka we have traditions for
everything ... how to eat, how to sleep, how to wear clothes.
For instance, we always keep our heads covered and always
wear a little prayer shawl ... This shows our constant
devotion to God. You may ask how did this tradition start.
I'll tell you -- I don't know. But it's a tradition ...
Because of our traditions, everyone knows who he is and what
God expects him to do.

TEVYE & PAPAS

(Sing)
WHO DAY AND NIGHT
MUST SCRAMBLE FOR A LIVING
FEED A WIFE AND CHILDREN
SAY HIS DAILY PRAYERS.
AND WHO HAS THE RIGHT
AS MASTER OF THE HOUSE
TO HAVE THE FINAL WORD AT HOME.

ALL

THE PAPA, THE PAPA ... TRADITION
THE PAPA, THE PAPA ... TRADITION

GOLDE & MAMAS

WHO MUST KNOW THE WAY TO MAKE A PROPER HOME
A QUIET HOME, A KOSHER HOME
WHO MUST RAISE A FAMILY AND RUN THE HOME
SO PAPA'S FREE TO READ THE HOLY BOOK.

ALL

THE MAMA, THE MAMA ... TRADITION
THE MAMA, THE MAMA ... TRADITION

                    SONS
AT THREE I STARTED HEBREW SCHOOL
AT TEN I LEARNED A TRADE
I HEAR THEY PICKED A BRIDE FOR ME
I HOPE ... SHE'S PRETTY.

                    ALL
THE SONS, THE SONS ... TRADITION
THE SONS, THE SONS ... TRADITION

                    DAUGHTERS
AND WHO DOES MAMA TEACH
TO MEND AND TEND AND FIX
PREPARING ME TO MARRY
WHOEVER PAPA PICKS?

                    ALL
THE DAUGHTERS, THE DAUGHTERS ... TRADITION
THE DAUGHTERS, THE DAUGHTERS ... TRADITION

     (Repeat as round)

                    PAPAS
THE PAPAS.

                    MAMAS
THE MAMAS.

                    SONS
THE SONS.

                    DAUGHTERS
THE DAUGHTERS.

                    ALL
TRADITION.

     (Repeat)

                    TEVYE
And in the circle of our little village, we have always had
on special types. For instance, Yente, the matchmaker ...

                    YENTE
Avram, I have a perfect match for your son. A wonderful
girl.

                    AVRAM
Who is it?

                    YENTE
Ruchel, the shoemaker's daughter.

                    4

                              AVRAM
Ruchel? But she can hardly see. She's almost blind.

                              YENTE
Tell the truth, Avram, is your son so much to look at? The
way she sees and the way he looks, it's a perfect match.

          (ALL dance)

                              TEVYE
And Nahum, the beggar ...

                              BEGGAR
ALMS for the poor, alms for the poor ...

                              LAZAR
Here, Reb Nahum, is one kopek.

                              BEGGAR
One kopek? Last week you gave me two kopeks.

                              LAZAR
I had a bad week.

                              BEGGAR
So, if you had a bad week, why should I suffer?

          (ALL dance)

                              TEVYE
And most important, our beloved Rabbi ...

                              MENDEL
Rabbi, may I ask you a question?

                              RABBI
Certainly, my son.

                              MENDEL
Is there a proper blessing for the tsar?

                              RABBI
A blessing for the tsar? Of course. May God bless and
keep the Tsar ... far away from us!

          (ALL dance)

                              TEVYE
Then, there are others in our village. They have a much
bigger circle.

               (PRIEST, CONSTABLE, OTHER RUSSIANS
               CROSS ... THE GROUPS nod to each
               other)

                               5

                        TEVYE (Continued)
His Honor the Constable, His Honor the Priest, and His
Honor ... many others. We don't bother them and so far
they don't bother us ... And among ourselves we get along
perfectly well. Of course, there was the time when he
sold him a horse and he delivered a mule, but that's all
settled now. Now we live in simple peace and harmony and ...

                (The TWO MEN begin an argument,
                Mule vs. Horse, which is taken
                up by the entire group)

                        1st MAN
It was a horse.

                        2nd MAN
It was a mule.

                        CHORUS
HORSE!

                        CHORUS
MULE!

                (Repeated)

                        TEVYE
                (Quieting them)
Tradition. Without our traditions, our lives would be as
shaky as ... as a fiddler on the roof!

Scene 1

Kitchen of TEVYE's house. GOLDE,
TZEITEL, and HODEL are preparing
for the Sabbath. SPHRINTZE and
BIELKE enter from outside, carrying
logs.

SHPRINTZE

Mama, where should we put these?

GOLDE

Put them on my head! By the stove, foolish girl.... Where
is Chava?

HODEL

She's in the barn, milking.

BIELKE

When will Papa be home?

GOLDE

It's almost Sabbath and he worries a lot when he'll be home!
All day long riding on top of his wagon like a prince.

TZEITEL

Mama, you know that Papa works hard.

GOLDE

His horse works harder! ... And you don't have to defend
your Papa to me. I know him longer than you. ... He could
drive a person crazy ... He should only live and be well ...
Shprintze, bring me some more potatoes.

(CHAVA enters, carrying a basket,
with a book under her apron)

Chava, did you finish milking?

CHAVA

Yes, Mama.
(SHE drops the book)

GOLDE

You were reading again? Why does a girl have to read? Will
it get her a better husband? Here.
(Hands CHAVA the book.

CHAVA exits into the house. SHPRINTZE
enters with basket of potatoes)

                         SHPRINTZE
Mama, Yente's coming. She's down the road.

                         HODEL
Maybe she's finally found a good match for you, Tzeitel.

                         GOLDE
From your mouth to God's ears.

                         TZEITEL
Why does she have to come now? It's almost Sabbath.

                         GOLDE
Go finish in the barn. I want to talk to Yente alone.

                         SHPRINTZE
Mama, can I go out and play?

                         GOLDE
You have feet? Go.

                         BIELKE
Can I go too?

                         GOLDE
Go too.

                         TZEITEL
But Mama, the men she finds. The last one was so old and
he was bald. He had no hair.

                         GOLDE
A poor girl without a dowry can't be so particular. You
want hair, marry a monkey.

                         TZEITEL
After all, Mama, I'm not yet twenty years old and ...

                         GOLDE
Shah!
          (Spits between fingers)
Do you have to boast about your age? Do you want to tempt
the Evil Eye? ... Inside.

          (TZEITEL enters the house as YENTE
          enters from outside)

                         YENTE
Golde Darling, I had to see you because I have such news for
you. And not just every day in the week news, once in a
lifetime news. And where are your daughters? Outside, no?
Good, such diamonds, such jewels. You'll see, Golde, I'll
find every one of them a husband. But you shouldn't be so
picky. ... Even the worst husband, God forbid, is better

                            8

                              YENTE (Continued)
than no husband, God forbid ... And who should know better
than me? Ever since my husband died I've been a poor widow,
alone, nobody to talk to, nothing to say to anyone. It's no
life. All I do at night is think of him, and even thinking
of him gives me no pleasure because, you know as well as I,
he was not much of a person ... Never made a living,
everything he touched turned to mud, but better than nothing.

                         MOTEL
              (Entering from door L)
Good evening. Is Tzeitel in the house?

                         GOLDE
But she's busy. You can come back later.

                         MOTEL
There's something I'd like to tell her.

                         GOLDE
Later.

                         TZEITEL
Oh, Motel, I thought I heard you.

                         GOLDE
Finish what you were doing.
              (To MOTEL)
I said later.

                         MOTEL
              (Exiting L)
All right!

                         YENTE
What does that poor little tailor Motel want with Tzeitel?

                         GOLDE
They have been friends since they were babies together.
They talk, they play ...

                         YENTE
              (Suspiciously)
They play? What do they play?

                         GOLDE
Who knows? They're just children ...

                         YENTE
From such children, come other children.

                         GOLDE
Motel he's a nothing, Yente, you said ...

                              9

                              YENTE
Ah, children, children! They are your blessing in your old
age. But my Aaron couldn't give me children. Believe me,
he was good as gold, never raised his voice to me, but
otherwise he was not much of a man, so what good is it if
he never raised his voice? But what's the use complaining,
other women enjoy complaining, but not Yente. Not every
woman in the world is a Yente. Well, I must prepare my poor
Sabbath table, so goodbye, Golde, and it was a pleasure
talking our hearts out to each other.
                    (SHE starts to exit)

                              GOLDE
Yente, you said you had news for me.

                              YENTE
Oh, I'm losing my head. One day it will fall off altogether,
and a horse will kick it into the mud and goodbye, Yente.
Of course, the news. It's about Lazar Wolf, the butcher.
A good man, a fine man. And I don't have to tell you that
he's well off. But he's lonely, the poor man. You understand? Of course you do. To make it short, out of the
whole town, he's cast his eye on Tzeitel ...

                              GOLDE
My Tzeitel?

                              YENTE
No, the Tzar's Tzeitel! Of course your Tzeitel.

                              GOLDE
Such a match, for my Tzeitel. But Tevye wants a learned
man, he doesn't like Lazar.

                              YENTE
Listen to me, Golde, send Tevye to him, don't tell him what
it's about, let Lazar discuss it himself, he'll win him
over, he's a good man, a wealthy man ... True? True. So
you'll tell me how it went, and you don't have to thank me,
Golde, because aside from my fee which anyway Lazar will
pay, it gives me satisfaction to make people happy, what
better satisfaction is there, so goodbye, Golde, and you're
welcome.
                    (YENTE exits door L)

                              TZEITEL
What did she want, Mama?

                              GOLDE
When I want you to know, I'll tell you ... Finish washing
the floor.
                    (SHE exits UC. HODEL and CHAVA enter
                    door R, with wash mop, bucket)

                               10

                         HODEL
I wonder if Yente found a husband for you?

                         TZEITEL
I'm not anxious for Yente to find me a husband.

                         CHAVA
Not unless it's Motel, the tailor.

                         TZEITEL
I didn't ask you.

                         HODEL
Tzeitel, you're the oldest. They have to make a match for
you before they can make one for me.

                         CHAVA
And then after her, one for me.

                         HODEL
So if Yente brings ...

                         TZEITEL
Oh, Yente ... Yente ...

                         HODEL
Well, somebody has to arrange the matches. Young people
can't decide these things for themselves.

                         CHAVA
She might bring someone wonderful ...

                         HODEL
Someone interesting ...

                         CHAVA
And well-off ...

                         HODEL
And important ...

        MATCHMAKER, MATCHMAKER
        MAKE ME A MATCH
        FIND ME A FIND
        CATCH ME A CATCH
        MATCHMAKER, MATCHMAKER
        LOOK THROUGH YOUR BOOK
        AND MAKE ME A PERFECT MATCH

                         CHAVA
        MATCHMAKER, MATCHMAKER
        I'LL BRING THE VEIL
        YOU BRING THE GROOM

SLENDER AND PALE
BRING ME A RING FOR I'M LONGING TO BE
THE ENVY OF ALL I SEE

HODEL

FOR PAPA,
MAKE HIM A SCHOLAR

CHAVA

FOR MAMA,
MAKE HIM RICH AS A KING

CHAVA & HODEL

FOR ME ... WELL ...
I WOULDN'T HOLLER
IF HE WERE AS HANDSOME AS ANYTHING.

MATCHMAKER, MATCHMAKER
MAKE ME A MATCH
FIND ME A FIND
CATCH ME A CATCH
NIGHT AFTER NIGHT IN THE DARK I'M ALONE
SO FIND ME A MATCH
OF MY OWN.

TZEITEL
(To CHAVA)
Since when are you interested in a match, Chava? I thought
you just had your eye on your books.

(HODEL chuckles)

And you have your eye on the Rabbi's son.

HODEL
Why not? We only have one Rabbi and he only has one son.
Why shouldn't I want the best?

TZEITEL
Because you're a girl from a poor family. So whatever Yente
brings, you'll take. Right? Of course, right.
(Sings)
HODEL, OH HODEL
HAVE I MADE A MATCH FOR YOU
HE'S HANDSOME, HE'S YOUNG!
ALL RIGHT, HE'S SIXTY-TWO
BUT HE'S A NICE MAN, A GOOD CATCH -- TRUE? TRUE.

I PROMISE YOU'LL BE HAPPY
AND EVEN IF YOU'RE NOT
THERE'S MORE TO LIFE THAN THAT
... DON'T ASK ME WHAT

TZEITEL (Continued)
CHAVA, I FOUND HIM
WILL YOU BE A LUCKY BRIDE
HE'S HANDSOME, HE'S TALL
THAT IS FROM SIDE TO SIDE.
FOR HE'S A NICE MAN, A GOOD CATCH.   RIGHT?   RIGHT.

YOU HEARD HE HAS A TEMPER
HE'LL BEAT YOU EVERY NIGHT
BUT ONLY WHEN HE'S SOBER
SO YOU'RE ALL RIGHT.

DID YOU THINK YOU'D GET A PRINCE?
WELL, I DO THE BEST I CAN
WITH NO DOWRY, NO MONEY, NO FAMILY BACKGROUND
BE GLAD YOU GOT A MAN ...

CHAVA
MATCHMAKER, MATCHMAKER
YOU KNOW THAT I'M
STILL VERY YOUNG
PLEASE ... TAKE YOUR TIME

HODEL
UP TO THIS MINUTE
I MISUNDERSTOOD
THAT I COULD GET STUCK FOR GOOD.

CHAVA & HODEL
DEAR YENTE
SEE THAT HE'S GENTLE
REMEMBER
YOU WERE ALSO A BRIDE
IT'S NOT ... THAT ...
I'M SENTIMENTAL
IT'S JUST THAT I'M TERRIFIED!

ALL
MATCHMAKER, MATCHMAKER
PLAN ME NO PLANS
I'M IN NO RUSH
MAYBE I'VE LEARNED
PLAYING WITH MATCHES
A GIRL CAN GET BURNED
SO
BRING ME NO RING
GROOM ME NO GROOM
FIND ME NO FIND
CATCH ME NO CATCH
UNLESS HE'S A MATCHLESS MATCH.

DIMOUT

ACT   I

Scene 2

Exterior of TEVYE's house. TEVYE
enters, pulling cart. HE stops DCS,
sits wagon seat.

TEVYE

Today I am a horse. ... Dear God, did you have to make my
poor old horse lose his shoe, just before the Sabbath? That
wasn't nice. ... It's enough you pick on me, Tevye ... bless
him with five daughters, a life of poverty. What have you
got against my horse? ... Sometimes I think when things are
too quiet up there, you say to yourself: Let's see, what
kind of mischief can I play on my friend, Tevye?

GOLDE
(Entering from house)
You're finally here, my breadwinner.

TEVYE
(Gestures to Heaven)
I'll talk to you later.

GOLDE

Where's your horse?

TEVYE

He was invited to the blacksmith's for the Sabbath.

GOLDE

Hurry up, the sun won't wait for you. I have something to
say to you.
(Exits into the house)

TEVYE

As the good book says, Heal us O Lord and we shall be healed.
In other words, send us the cure, we've got the sickness
already. ... I'm not really complaining -- after all, with
your help, I'm starving to death. You made many, many poor
people. I realize, of course, that it's no shame to be poor,
but it's no great honor either. So what would have been so
terrible if I had a small fortune?

IF I WERE A RICH MAN
DAIDLE, DEEDLE DAIDLE
DIGGUH DIGGUH DEEDLE DAIDLE DUM
ALL DAY LONG I'D BIDDY BIDDY BUM
IF I WERE A WEALTHY MAN

14

WOULDN'T HAVE TO WORK HARD
DAIDLE DEEDLE DAIDLE
DIGGUH DIGGUH DEEDLE DAIDLE DUM
IF I WERE A BIDDY BIDDY RICH
DIGGUH DIGGUH DEEDLE DAIDLE MAN

I'D BUILD A BIG TALL HOUSE WITH ROOMS BY THE DOZEN
RIGHT IN THE MIDDLE OF THE TOWN
A FINE TIN ROOF WITH REAL WOODEN FLOORS BELOW
THERE WOULD BE ONE LONG STAIRCASE JUST GOING UP
AND ONE EVEN LONGER COMING DOWN
AND ONE MORE LEADING NOWHERE JUST FOR SHOW

I'D FILL MY YARD WITH CHICKS AND TURKEYS AND GEESE
AND DUCKS FOR THE TOWN TO SEE AND HEAR
SQUAWKING JUST AS NOISILY AS THEY CAN
AND EACH LOUD QUACK AND CLUCK AND GOBBLE AND HONK
WILL LAND LIKE A TRUMPET ON THE EAR
AS IF TO SAY HERE LIVES A WEALTHY MAN

IF I WERE A RICH MAN, ETC.

I SEE MY WIFE, MY GOLDE, LOOKING LIKE A RICH MAN'S WIFE
WITH A PROPER DOUBLE CHIN
SUPERVISING MEALS TO HER HEART'S DELIGHT
I SEE HER PUTTING ON AIRS AND STRUTTING LIKE A PEACOCK
OI! WHAT A HAPPY MOOD SHE'S IN
SCREAMING AT THE SERVANTS DAY AND NIGHT.

THE MOST IMPORTANT MEN IN TOWN WILL COME TO FAWN ON ME
THEY WILL ASK ME TO ADVISE THEM LIKE SOLOMON THE WISE
"IF YOU PLEASE, REB TEVYE ... PARDON ME, REB TEVYE ..."
POSING PROBLEMS THAT WOULD CROSS A RABBI'S EYES.
        (HE chants)
AND IT WON'T MAKE ONE BIT OF DIFF'RENCE
IF I ANSWER RIGHT OR WRONG
WHEN YOU'RE RICH THEY THINK YOU REALLY KNOW!

IF I WERE RICH I'D HAVE THE TIME THAT I LACK
TO SIT IN THE SYNAGOGUE AND PRAY
AND MAYBE HAVE A SEAT BY THE EASTERN WALL
AND I'D DISCUSS THE HOLY BOOKS WITH THE LEARNED MEN
SEVEN HOURS EVERY DAY
THIS WOULD BE THE SWEETEST THING OF ALL ...
        (Sigh)
IF I WERE A RICH MAN
DAIDLE DEEDLE DAIDLE
DIGGUH DIGGUH DEEDLE DAIDLE DUM
ALL DAY LONG I'D BIDDY BIDDY BUM
IF I WERE A WEALTHY MAN

WOULDN'T HAVE TO WORK HARD
DAIDLE DEEDLE DAIDLE
DIGGUH DIGGUH DEEDLE DAIDLE DUM ...

TEVYE (Continued)
LORD, WHO MADE THE LION AND THE LAMB
YOU DECREED I SHOULD BE WHAT I AM
WOULD IT SPOIL SOME VAST, ETERNAL PLAN ...
IF I WERE A WEALTHY MAN?

(As song ends, INNKEEPER, MENDEL,
AVRAM and OTHERS enter)

INNKEEPER
There he is! ... You forgot my order for the Sabbath!

TEVYE
Reb Mordcha, I had a little accident with my horse.

MENDEL
Tevye, you didn't bring the Rabbi's order.

TEVYE
I know, Reb Mendel.

AVRAM
Tevye, you forgot my order for the Sabbath.

TEVYE
This is bigger news than the plague in Odessa.

AVRAM
Talking about news, terrible news in the outside world ...
terrible.

INNKEEPER
What is it?

MENDEL
What does it say?

AVRAM
In a village called Rajanka, all the Jews were evicted,
forced to leave their homes ...

(ALL look at each other)

MENDEL
For what reason?

AVRAM
It doesn't say. Maybe the Tsar wanted their land ... maybe
a plague ...

INNKEEPER
May the Tsar have his own personal plague.

16

                              ALL
Amen.

                            MENDEL
          (To AVRAM)
Why don't you ever bring us some good news?

                            AVRAM
I only read it. It was an edict from the authorities.

                          INNKEEPER
May the authorities start itching in places that they can't
reach.

                              ALL
Amen.

                          PERCHIK
Why do you curse them? What good does your cursing do? ...
You stand around and curse and chatter and don't do any-
thing. You'll all chatter your way into the grave.

                            MENDEL
Excuse me, you're not from this village.

                          PERCHIK
No.

                            MENDEL
And where are you from?

                          PERCHIK
Kiev. ... I was a student in the University there.

                          INNKEEPER
Aha! The University. Is that where you learned to
criticize your elders?

                          PERCHIK
That's where I learned that there is more to life than talk.
You should know what's going on in the outside world.

                          INNKEEPER
Why should I break my head about the outside world? Let
them break their own heads.

                            TEVYE
He's right. ... As the good book says, if you spit in the
air, it lands in your face.

                          PERCHIK
That's nonsense. You can't close your eyes to what's
happening in the world.

                              17

                              TEVYE
He's right.

                              AVRAM
He's right and he's right? How can they both be right?

                              TEVYE
You know, you are also right.

                              INNKEEPER
He's right! He's still wet behind the ears! Good Sabbath,
Tevye.

                         AVRAM & OTHERS
Good Sabbath, Tevye.

                    (THEY take their orders and
                    leave. MENDEL remains)

                              MENDEL
Tevye, the Rabbi's order. My cheese!

                              TEVYE
Of course. So you're from Kiev, Reb ...

                              PERCHIK
Perchik.

                              TEVYE
Perchik. So, you're a newcomer here. As Abraham said,
"I am a stranger in a strange land."

                              MENDEL
Moses said that.

                              TEVYE
Forgive me. As King David put it, "I am slow of speech
and slow of tongue."

                              MENDEL
That was also Moses.

                              TEVYE
For a man with a slow tongue, he talked a lot.

                              MENDEL
And the cheese!

                    (TEVYE notices that PERCHIK
                    is eyeing the cheese hungrily)

                              TEVYE
Here, have a piece.

                    PERCHIK
I have no money. And I am not a beggar.

                    TEVYE
Here ... It's a blessing for me to give.

                    PERCHIK
Very well ... for your sake!
          (HE takes the cheese and devours
          it)

                    TEVYE
Thank you ... you know, it's no crime to be poor.

                    PERCHIK
In this world, it's the rich who are the criminals. Some
day their wealth will be ours.

                    TEVYE
That would be nice. If they would agree, I would agree.

                    MENDEL
And who will make this miracle come to pass?

                    PERCHIK
People. Ordinary people.

                    MENDEL
Like you?

                    PERCHIK
Like me?

                    MENDEL
Nonsense!

                    TEVYE
... And until your golden day comes, Reb Perchik, how will
you live?

                    PERCHIK
By giving lessons to children ... Do you have children?

                    TEVYE
I have five daughters.

                    TEVYE
I have five daughters.

                    PERCHIK
Five?

                    TEVYE
Daughters.

                        PERCHIK
Girls should learn too. Girls are people.

                        MENDEL
A radical!

                        PERCHIK
I would be willing to teach them. Open their minds to
great thoughts.

                        TEVYE
What great thoughts?

                        PERCHIK
Well, the Bible has many lessons for our times.

                        TEVYE
I am a very poor man. Food for lessons? Good.

          (PERCHIK nods)

Stay with us for the Sabbath. Of course, we don't eat
like kings, but we don't starve either. As the good book
says, when a poor man eats a chicken, one of them is sick."

                        MENDEL
Where does the book say that?

                        TEVYE
Well, it doesn't exactly say that, but someplace it has
something about a chicken. ... Good Sabbath.

                        MENDEL
Good Sabbath.

                        PERCHIK
Good Sabbath.

               (THEY exit as TEVYE and PERCHIK
               enter house)

ACT   I

Scene 3

Interior of TEVYE's house.
TEVYE and PERCHIK enter.

TEVYE

Good Sabbath, children.

CHILDREN
(Running to him)
Good Sabbath, Papa.

TEVYE

Children!

(THEY all stop)

... This is Perchik. Perchik, this is my oldest daugher.

PERCHIK

Good Sabbath.

TZEITEL

Good Sabbath.

PERCHIK
You have a pleasant daughter.

TEVYE
I have five pleasant daughters.

(HE beckons to them and THEY
run into his arms, eagerly, and
TEVYE kisses each, upstage to
downstage)

This is mine ... this is mine ... this is mine ... this
is mine ...

(MOTEL enters -- TEVYE almost
kisses him in sequence)

This is not mine. ... Perchik, this is Motel Kamzoil
and he is ...

GOLDE
(Entering)
So you did me a favor and came in.

21

                         GOLDE
              (Entering)
So you did me a favor and came in.

                         TEVYE
This is also mine. Golde, this is Perchik, from Kiev,
and he is staying the Sabbath with us. He is a teacher.
              (To SHPRINTZE and BIELKE)
Would you like to take lessons from him?

                         PERCHIK
I am really a good teacher ... A very good teacher.

                         HODEL
I heard once, the Rabbi who must praise himself has a
congregation of one.

                         PERCHIK
Your daughter has a quick and witty tongue.

                         TEVYE
The wit she gets from me. As the Good Book says ...

                         GOLDE
The Good Book can wait. Get washed!

                         TEVYE
The tongue she gets from her mother.

                         GOLDE
Motel, you're also eating with us?

              (MOTEL gestures "Yes, if I may")

Of course, another blessing. Tzeitel, two more.
Shprintze, Bielke, get washed ...

                         TZEITEL
Motel can help me.

                         GOLDE
Get the table. All right. Chava, you go too.
              (To PERCHIK)
You can wash outside at the well.
              (To TEVYE)
Tevye, I have something to say to you.

                         TEVYE
Why should today be different?
              (HE starts to pray)

                         GOLDE
Tevye, I have to tell you ...

                              TEVYE
Shhh. I'm praying ...
          (Prays)

                              GOLDE
Lazar Wolf wants to see you.

               (TEVYE begins praying again,
               stopping only to respond to
               GOLDE, then returning to prayer)

                              TEVYE
The butcher? About what?
          (Prays)

                              GOLDE
I don't know. Only that he says it is important.

                              TEVYE
What can be important? I have nothing for him to
slaughter.
          (Prays)

                              GOLDE
After the Sabbath, see him and talk to him.

                              TEVYE
Talk to him about what? If he is thinking about buying
my new milk cow ...
          (Prays)
... he can forget it.
          (Prays)

                              GOLDE
Tevye, don't be an ox. A man sends an important message,
at least you can talk to him.

                              TEVYE
Talk about what? He wants my new milk cow!
          (Prays)

                              GOLDE
Talk to him!

                              TEVYE
All right. After the Sabbath, I'll talk to him.

               (HE and GOLDE exit -- HE is still
               praying. MOTEL, TZEITEL and CHAVA
               bring the table into the house.
               CHAVA exits)

                    TZEITEL
Motel, Yente was here.

                              23

MOTEL

I saw her.

TZEITEL

If they agree on someone there will be a match and then
it will be too late for us.

MOTEL

Don't worry Tzeitel. I have found someone who will sell
me his used sewing machine, so in a few weeks I'll have
saved up enough to buy it and then your Father will be
impressed with me.

TZEITEL

But Motel, a few weeks may be too late.

MOTEL

But what else can we do?

TZEITEL

You could ask my father for my hand tonite. Now!

MOTEL

Why should he consider me now? I'm only a poor tailer?

TZEITEL

And I'm only the daughter of a poor milkman. Just talk
to him.

MOTEL

Tzeitel, if your father says no, that's it, it's final ...
He'll yell at me.

TZEITEL

Motel!

MOTEL

I'm just a poor tailor.

TZEITEL

Motel, even a poor tailor is entitled to some happiness.

MOTEL

That's true.

TZEITEL

Will you talk to him? Will you talk to him?

MOTEL

All right, I'll talk to him.

TEVYE
            (Entering)
It's late! Where is everybody? Late.

                    MOTEL
Reb Tevye ...

                    TEVYE
Come in, children, we're lighting the candles.

                    MOTEL
Reb Tevye ...
          (Repeats, summoning courage)

                    TEVYE
Yes? What is it? ...
          (Loudly)
Well, Motel, what is it?

                    MOTEL
Good Sabbath, Reb Tevye.

                    TEVYE
Good Sabbath, Good Sabbath ... Come children, come.

          (FAMILY, PERCHIK, MOTEL gather
          around table.

          GOLDE lights candles, says
          prayer under her breath)

          "SABBATH PRAYER"

                    TEVYE & GOLDE
MAY THE LORD PROTECT AND DEFEND YOU
MAY HE ALWAYS SHIELD YOU FROM SHAME
MAY YOU COME TO BE
IN YISROEL A SHINING NAME
MAY YOU BE LIKE RUTH AND LIKE ESTHER
MAY YOU BE DESERVING OF PRAISE
STRENGHTHEN THEM, OH LORD
AND KEEP THEM FROM THE STRANGER'S WAYS

MAY GOD BLESS YOU
AND GRANT YOU LONG LIVES

                    GOLDE
MAY THE LORD FULFILL OUR SABBATH PRAYER FOR YOU

                    BOTH
MAY GOD MAKE YOU
GOOD MOTHERS AND WIVES

                    TEVYE
MAY HE SEND YOU HUSBANDS WHO WILL CARE FOR YOU

                    BOTH
MAY THE LORD PROTECT AND DEFEND YOU

                    25

BOTH (Continued)
MAY THE LORD PRESERVE YOU FROM PAIN
FAVOR THEM, OH LORD
WITH HAPPINESS AND PEACE
OH, HEAR OUR SABBATH PRAYER
AMEN.

DIMOUT

SL
With
Mama & Papa

ACT I

Scene 4

The Inn, the following evening.
Several people are sitting at
tables, AVRAM, MENDEL, etc. LAZAR
is waiting impatiently, drumming on
the tabletop, watching the door.

                    LAZAR
Reb Mordcha.

                    INNKEEPER
Yes, Lazar Wolf.

                    LAZAR
Please bring me a bottle of your best brandy and two glasses

                    AVRAM
Your best brandy, Reb Lazar.

                    INNKEEPER
What's the occasion? Are you getting ready for a party?

                    LAZAR
There might be a party. Maybe even a wedding.

                    INNKEEPER
A wedding? Wonderful. And I'll be happy to make the
wedding merry, lead the dancing and so forth. For a little
fee, naturally.

                    LAZAR
Naturally, a wedding is no wedding without you -- and your
fee.

          (RUSSIANS enter)

                    RUSSIAN
Good evening, Innkeeper.

                    INNKEEPER
Good evening.

                    RUSSIAN
We'd like a drink. Sit down, Fyedka.

                    INNKEEPER
Vodka? Schnapps?

                         RUSSIAN (FYEDKA)
Vodka.

                         INNKEEPER
Right away.

          (TEVYE enters. LAZAR, who has been
          watching the door, turns away,
          unconcernedly)

                         TEVYE
Good evening.

                         INNKEEPER
Good evening, Tevye.

                         MENDEL
What are you doing here so early?

                         TEVYE
He wants to buy my new milk cow. Good evening, Reb Lazar.

                         LAZAR
Ah, Tevye -- sit down. Have a drink.
          (Pours drink)

                         TEVYE
I won't insult you by saying no.
          (Drinks)

                         LAZAR
How goes it with you, Tevye?

                         TEVYE
How should it go?

                         LAZAR
You're right.

                         TEVYE
And you?

                         LAZAR
The same.

                         TEVYE
I'm sorry to hear that.

                         LAZAR
          (Pours drink)
So how's your brother-in-law in America?

                         TEVYE
I believe he is doing very well.

28

                         LAZAR
He wrote you?

                         TEVYE
Not lately.

                         LAZAR
Then how do you know?

                         TEVYE
If he was doing badly he would write. May I?

                         LAZAR
Tevye -- I suppose you know why I wanted to see you.

                         TEVYE
                    (Drinks)
Yes, I do, Reb Lazar, but there is no use talking about it.

                         LAZAR
                    (Upset)
Why not?

                         TEVYE
Why yes? Why should I get rid of her?

                         LAZAR
Well, you have a few more without her.

                         TEVYE
I see! Today you want one. Tomorrow you may want two.

                         LAZAR
Two? What would I do with two??

                         TEVYE
The same as you do with one!

                         LAZAR
Tevye, this is very important to me.

                         TEVYE
Why is it so important to you?

                         LAZAR
Frankly ... because I am lonesome.

                         TEVYE
Lonesome? What are you talking about?

                         LAZAR
You don't know?

TEVYE

We're talking about my new milk cow. The one you want to
buy from me.

LAZAR
(Stares at TEVYE, then bursts
into laughter)
A milk cow! So I won't be lonesome!
(HE howls with laughter.

TEVYE stares at him)

TEVYE

What's so funny?

LAZAR

I was talking about your daughter. Your daughter Tzeitel!
(Bursts into laughter.

TEVYE stares at him, upset)

TEVYE

My daughter Tzeitel?
(Turns to audience)

LAZAR

Of course, your daughter, Tzeitel! I see her in my butcher
shop every Thursday. She's made a good impression on me ...
I like her ... And as for me, Tevye ... as you know, I'm
pretty well off. I have my own house, a good store, a
servant ... Look, Tevye, why do we have to try to impress
each other? Let's shake hands and call it a match. And you
won't need a dowry for her. And maybe you'll find something
in your own purse, too ...

TEVYE
(Shouts)
Shame on you! Shame!
(Hic)
What do you mean ... my purse? My Tzeitel is not the sort
that I would sell for money!

LAZAR

All right! Just as you say. We won't talk about money.
The main thing is, let's get it done with. And I will be
good to her, Tevye.
(Slightly embarrassed)
I like her ... What do you think?

(MUSICIANS appear)

30

                              TEVYE
                    (To audience)
What do I think? What do I think? I never liked him! Why
should I? ... You can have a fine conversation with him if
you talk about kidneys and livers ... On the other hand,
not everybody has to be a scholar? If you're wealthy
enough, no one will call you stupid ... And with a butcher,
my daughter will surely never know hunger. Of course, he
has a problem -- he's much older than her. That's her
problem. But she's younger. That's his problem. ... I
always thought of him as a butcher, but I misjudged him. He
is a good man, he likes her, he will try to make her happy.
                    (Turns to LAZAR)
What do I think? It's a match.

                              LAZAR
                    (Delighted)
You agree?

                              TEVYE
I agree.

                              LAZAR
Oh, Tevye, that's wonderful. Let's drink on it.

                              TEVYE
Why not? To you.

                              LAZAR
No, my friend, to you.

                              TEVYE
To the both of us.

                              LAZAR
To our agreement.

                              TEVYE
To our agreement. To our prosperity. To good health and
happiness. And most important,
                    (Sings)

     TO LIFE, TO LIFE, L'CHAIM

                              BOTH
                    (Sing)
     L'CHAIM. L'CHAIM, TO LIFE

                              TEVYE
     HERE'S TO THE FATHER, I'VE TRIED TO BE

                              LAZAR
     HERE'S TO MY BRIDE TO BE

                               31

                    BOTH
        DRINK, L'CHAIM, TO LIFE, TO LIFE, L'CHAIM
        L'CHAIM, L'CHAIM, TO LIFE

                    TEVYE
        LIFE HAS A WAY OF CONFUSING US

                    LAZAR
        BLESSING AND BRUISING US

                    BOTH
        DRINK, L'CHAIM, TO LIFE.

                    TEVYE
        GOD WOULD LIKE US TO BE JOYFUL
        EVEN WHEN OUR HEARTS LIE PANTING ON THE FLOOR

                    LAZAR
        HOW MUCH MORE CAN WE BE JOYFUL
        WHEN THERE'S REALLY SOMETHING
        TO BE JOYFUL FOR

                    BOTH
        TO LIFE, TO LIFE, L'CHAIM

                    TEVYE
        TO TZEITEL, MY DAUGHTER

                    LAZAR
        MY WIFE
        IT GIVES YOU SOMETHING TO THINK ABOUT

                    TEVYE
        SOMETHING TO DRINK ABOUT

                    BOTH
        DRINK, L'CHAIM, TO LIFE.

                    LAZAR
Reb Mordcha.

                    INNKEEPER
Yes, Lazar Wolf.

                    LAZAR
Drinks for everybody.

                    MENDEL
What's the occasion?

                         LAZAR
I'm taking myself a bride.

                         ALL
Who? ... Who?

                         LAZAR
Tevye's eldest, Tzeitel.

                         ALL
Mazeltove ... wonderful ... congratulations, etc.

        (Sing)

    TO LAZAR WOLF

                         TEVYE
    TO TEVYE

                         ALL
    TO TZEITEL, YOUR DAUGHTER

                         LAZAR
    MY WIFE

                         ALL
    MAY ALL YOUR FUTURES BE PLEASANT ONES
    NOT LIKE OUR PRESENT ONES
    DRINK, L'CHAIM, TO LIFE
    TO LIFE, L'CHAIM
    L'CHAIM, L'CHAIM, TO LIFE
    IT TAKES A WEDDING TO MAKE US SAY
    LET'S LIVE ANOTHER DAY
    DRINK, L'CHAIM, TO LIFE

    WE'LL RAISE A GLASS AND SIP A DROP OF SCHNAPPS
    IN HONOR OF THE GREAT GOOD LUCK
    THAT FAVORED YOU.

    WE KNOW THAT
    WHEN GOOD FORTUNE FAVORS TWO SUCH MEN
    IT STANDS TO REASON WE DESERVE IT TOO
    TO US AND OUR GOOD FORTUNE
    BE HAPPY, BE HEALTHY, LONG LIFE
    AND IF OUR GOOD FORTUNE NEVER COMES
    HERE'S TO WHATEVER COMES
    DRINK, L'CHAIM, TO LIFE

    DAI-DAI-DAI-DAI-DAI-DAI-DAI, ETC.

        (Begin dance)

                    RUSSIAN
ZACHAVA ZDAROVIA
HEAVEN BLESS YOU BOTH NAZDROVIA
TO YOUR HEALTH AND MAY WE LIVE TOGETHER IN PEACE.

ZACHAVA ZDAROVIA
HEAVEN BLESS YOU BOTH NAZDROVIA
TO YOUR HEALTH AND MAY WE LIVE TOGETHER IN PEACE.

                    OTHER RUSSIANS
ZACHAVA ZDAROVIA
HEAVEN BLESS YOU BOTH NAZDROVIA
TO YOUR HEALTH AND MAY WE LIVE TOGETHER IN PEACE.

        (RUSSIANS begin dance, OTHERS join
        in, dance to wild finale pile-up on
        bar)

                    TEVYE
To Life!

                    BLACKOUT

                    34

Scene 5

Street outside the Inn. Entering
from Inn door are FIDDLER, LAZAR,
TEVYE, and others, singing "To Life.

                    LAZAR
You know, Tevye, after the marriage, we will be related. You
will be my papa.

                    TEVYE
Your papa! I always wanted a son, but one a little younger
than myself ...

          (CONSTABLE enters)

                    CONSTABLE
Good evening.

                    RUSSIAN
Good evening, Constable.

                    CONSTABLE
What's the celebration?

                    RUSSIAN
Tevye' is marrying off his oldest daughter.

                    CONSTABLE
May I offer my congratulations, Tevye.

                    TEVYE
Thank you, your honor.

                    CONSTABLE
Oh, Tevye, I have a piece of news that I think I should
tell you, as a friend.

                    TEVYE
Yes, your honor?

                    CONSTABLE
And I'm giving you this news because I like you. You are a
decent, honest person, even though you are a Jewish dog.

                    TEVYE
Thank you, your honor. How often does a man get a
compliment like that? And your news?

CONSTABLE

We have received orders that sometime soon this district is
to have a little unofficial demonstration.

TEVYE

A pogrom? Here?

CONSTABLE

No -- just a little unofficial demonstration.

TEVYE

How little?

CONSTABLE

Not too serious -- just some mischief, so that if an
inspector comes through, he will see that we have done our
duty. Personally, I don't know why there has to be this
trouble between people, but I thought I should tell you and
you can tell the others.

TEVYE

Thank you, your honor. You're a good man. If I may say so,
it's too bad you're not a Jew.

CONSTABLE

That's what I like about you, Tevye. Always joking. ...
And congratulations again, for your daughter.

TEVYE

Thank you, your honor. Goodbye.

(CONSTABLE exits R)

Dear God, why did you have to send me news like that, today
of all days? It's true that we are the chosen people. But
once in a while can't you choose someone else? ... Anyway,
thank you for sending a husband for my Tzeitel ... L'Chaim.

(FIDDLER enters, circles TEVYE, and
they dance off together)

DIMOUT

Scene 6

PERCHIK is teaching SHPRINTZE and
BIELKE while they peel potatoes at
a bench, R. HODEL is cleaning pails
at the pump, L.

PERCHIK

Now, children, I will tell you the story from the Bible of
Laban and Jacob, and then we will discuss it together. All
right?

(THEY nod)

Good -- now Laban had two daughters, Leah and the beautiful
Rachel. And Jacob loved the younger, Rachel, and he asked
Laban for her hand, Laban agreed, if Jacob would work for
him for seven years.

SHPRINTZE

Was Laban a mean man?

PERCHIK

He was an employer! ... Now, after Jacob worked seven years,
do you know what happened? Laban fooled him, and gave him
his ugly daughter, Leah. So, to marry Rachel, Jacob was
forced to work another seven years. You see, children, the
Bible clearly teaches us, you must never trust an employer
... Do you understand?

SHPRINTZE

Yes, Perchik.

BIELKE

Yes, Perchik.

PERCHIK

Good, now ...

GOLDE
(Entering from the Barn)
Papa isn't up yet?

HODEL

No, Mama.

GOLDE

Then enough lessons. We have to do Papa's work today.
How long can he sleep? He staggered home last night and
fell into bed like a dead man. I couldn't get a word out
of him. Put that away and clean the barn.

37

GOLDE (Continued)

(SHPRINTZE and BIELKE exit into
the barn)

Call me when Papa gets up.

(HODEL pumps bucket of water)

HODEL
That was a very interesting lesson, Perchik.

PERCHIK
Do you think so?

HODEL
Although I don't know if the Rabbi would agree with your
interpretation.

PERCHIK
And neither, I suppose, would the Rabbi's son.

HODEL
(Looking at CHAVA, who is
churning butter nearby)
My little sisters have big tongues.

(CHAVA exits with stool and
churn, left)

PERCHIK
And what do you know about him, except that he is the Rabbi's
son? Would you be interested in him if he were the
shoemaker's son, or the tinsmith's son?

HODEL
At least I know this ... he does not have any strange ideas
about turning the world upside down.

PERCHIK
Certainly. Any new idea would be strange to you. Remember,
the Lord said, "Let there be light."

HODEL
Yes, but He was not talking to you personally ...

PERCHIK
You have spirit. Even a little intelligence, perhaps.

HODEL
Thank you.

                    PERCHIK
But what good is your brain? Without curiosity it is a
rusty tool. Good day, Hodel.

                    HODEL
We have an old custom here. A boy acts respectfully to a
girl. But, of course, that is too traditional for an
advanced thinker like you.

                    PERCHIK
Our traditions! Nothing must change! Everything is perfect
exactly the way it is!

                    HODEL
We like our ways.

                    PERCHIK
Our ways are changing all over but here. Here men and
women must keep apart. Men study, women in the kitchen.
Boys and girls must not touch, should not even look at
each other.

                    HODEL
I am looking at you!

                    PERCHIK
You are very brave! ... Do you know that in the city boys
and girls can be affectionate without permission of a
matchmaker? They hold hands together, they even dance
together ... new dances ... like this.

          (Dance)

I learned it in Kiev ... Do you like it?

                    HODEL
It's very nice.

                    PERCHIK
There. We've just changed an old custom.

                    HODEL
Yes, well, you're welcome -- I mean, thank you -- I mean
good day ...

                    PERCHIK
Good day!

                    TEVYE
          (Enters above pump)
Bielke, Shprintze, what's your name?

                    HODEL
Hodel, Papa.

                              39

                              TEVYE
Where is Tzeitel?

                              HODEL
She's in the barn.

                              TEVYE
Call her out.

          (HODEL exits into barn)

Reb Perchik. How did the lesson go today?

                              PERCHIK
               (Watching HODEL's exit)
I think we made a good beginning.

                              GOLDE
Ah, he's finally up. What happened last night, besides your
drinking like a peasant? Did you see Lazar Wolf? What did
he say? What did you say? Do you have news?

                              TEVYE
Patience, woman. As the Good Book says, good news will
stay and bad news will refuse to leave. And there's
another saying that goes ...

                              GOLDE
You can die from such a man!

          (TZEITEL enters from barn. HODEL
          and CHAVA follow her out) Enter

                              TEVYE
Ah, Tzeitel, my lamb, come here ... Tzeitel, you are to be
congratulated. You are going to be married!

                              GOLDE
Married!

                              TZEITEL
What do you mean, Papa?

                              TEVYE
Lazar Wolf has asked for your hand.

                              GOLDE
I knew it!

                              TZEITEL
          (Bewildered)
The butcher?

                              40

GOLDE
        (Enraptured)
My heart told me this was our lucky day. O dear God, I
thank thee, I thank thee ...

                        TEVYE
And what do you say, Tzeitel?

                        GOLDE
What can she say? My first born, a bride. May you grow old
with him in fortune and honor ... not like Fruma-Sarah, that
first wife of his. She was a bitter woman, may she rest in
peace. Not like my Tzeitel. And now I must thank Yente.
My Tzeitel, a bride.
        (SHE hurries off)   Then

                HODEL/CHAVA
Mazeltov, Tzeitel.

        (THEY exit R)   then   Mazeltov

                        TEVYE
You call that a mazeltov? And you, Reb Perchik, aren't you
going to congratulate her?

                        PERCHIK
Congratulations, Tzeitel, for getting a rich man.

                        TEVYE
Again with the rich! What's wrong with being rich?

                        PERCHIK
It is no reason to marry. Money is the world's curse.

                        TEVYE
May the Lord smite me with it! And may I never recover!
Tzeitel knows I mean only her welfare. Am I right, Tzeitel?

                        TZEITEL
Yes, Papa.

                        TEVYE
You see.

                        PERCHIK
I see. I see very well.

                        TEVYE
Well, Tzeitel, my child, why are you so silent? Aren't
you happy with this blessing?

                        TZEITEL
        (Bursts into tears)
Oh, Papa, Papa ...

                        41

                        TEVYE
What is it? Tell me?

                        TZEITEL
Papa, I don't want to marry him. I can't marry him. I
can't ...

                        TEVYE
What do you mean, you can't? If I say you will, you will.

                        TZEITEL
Papa, if it's a matter of money, I'll do anything. I'll
hire myself out as a servant. I'll dig ditches, I'll haul
rocks, only don't make me marry him, Papa, please.

                        TEVYE
What's wrong with Lazar? He likes you.

                        TZEITEL
Papa, I will be unhappy with him. All my life will be
unhappy. I'll dig ditches, I'll haul rocks.

                        TEVYE
But we made an agreement. With us an agreement is an
agreement.

                        TZEITEL
Is that more important than I am, Papa? Papa, don't force
me. I'll be unhappy all my days.

                        TEVYE
All right ... I won't force you.

                        TZEITEL
Oh, thank you, Papa.

                        TEVYE
It seems it was not ordained that you should have all the
comforts of life, or that we should have a little joy in our
old age after all our hard work.

                        MOTEL
              (Enters, breathless)
Reb Tevye, may I speak to you?

                        TEVYE
Later, Motel. Later.

                        MOTEL
I would like to speak to you.

                        TEVYE
Not now, Motel, I have problems.

                              MOTEL
That's what I want to speak to you about. I think I can
help.

                              TEVYE
Certainly. Like a bandage can help a corpse. Goodbye,
Motel. Goodbye.

                              TZEITEL
At least listen to him, Papa.

                              TEVYE
All right. You have a tongue, talk.

                              MOTEL
Reb Tevye, I hear you are arranging a match for Tzeitel.

                              TEVYE
He also has ears.

                              MOTEL
I have a match for Tzeitel.

                              TEVYE
What kind of match?

                              MOTEL
A perfect fit.

                              TEVYE
A perfect fit.

                              MOTEL
Like a glove.

                              TEVYE
Like a glove.

                              MOTEL
This match was made exactly to measure.

                              TEVYE
A perfect fit. Made to measure. Stop talking like a
tailor and tell me who is it.

                              MOTEL
Please, don't shout at me.

                              TEVYE
All right. Who is it?

                              MOTEL
Who is it?

                               43

                              TEVYE
Who is it?

                              MOTEL
Who is it?

                              TEVYE
Who is it?

                              MOTEL
It's me ... myself.

                              TEVYE
          (Stares at him, then to audience,
          startled and amused)
Him? Himself?
          (To MOTEL)
Either you're completely out of your mind or you're crazy.
          (To audience)
He must be crazy.
          (To MOTEL)
Arranging a match for yourself. What are you, everything?
The bridegroom, the matchmaker, the guests all rolled into
one? I suppose you'll even perform the ceremony ...
          (To MOTEL)
You must be crazy.

                              MOTEL
Please don't shout at me, Reb Tevye. As for being my own
matchmaker -- I know it's a little unusual.

                              TEVYE
Unusual? It's crazy.

                              MOTEL
Times are changing, Reb Tevye. The thing is, your daughter
Tzeitel and I gave each other our pledge over than a year
ago that we would marry.

                              TEVYE
          (Stunned)
You gave each other a pledge?

                              TZEITEL
Yes, Papa, we gave each other our pledge.

                              TEVYE
          (Looks at them, turns to audience,
          sings)
     THEY GAVE EACH OTHER A PLEDGE
     UNHEARD OF, ABSURD.

                         TEVYE (Continued)
YOU GAVE EACH OTHER A PLEDGE
UNTHINKABLE.
WHERE DO YOU THINK YOU ARE?
IN MOSCOW?
IN PARIS?
WHERE DO THEY THINK THEY ARE?
AMERICA?
AND WHAT DO YOU THINK YOU'RE DOING?
YOU A STITCHER, YOU A NOTHING
WHO DO YOU THINK YOU ARE?
KING SOLOMON?
THIS ISN'T THE WAY IT'S DONE
NOT HERE, NOT NOW.
SOME THINGS I WILL NOT, I CANNOT ALLOW.
TRADITION
MARRIAGES MUST BE ARRANGED BY THE PAPA
THIS SHOULD NEVER BE CHANGED.
ONE LITTLE TIME YOU PULL OUT A PROP
AND WHERE DOES IT STOP?
WHERE DOES IT STOP?

             (Spoken)
Where does it stop? ... Do I still have something to say
about my daughter, or doesn't anyone have to ask a father
anymore?

                         MOTEL
I have wanted to ask you for some time, Reb Tevye, but first
I wanted to save up for my own sewing machine ...

                         TEVYE
Stop talking nonsense. You're just a poor tailor.

                         MOTEL
That's true, Reb Tevye, but even a poor tailor is entitled
to some happiness. I promise you, Reb Tevye, your daughter
will not starve.

                         TEVYE
             (Impressed, turns to audience)
He's beginning to talk like a man ... On the other hand,
what kind of match would that be, with a poor tailor? ...
On the other hand, he's an honest, hard worker ... On the
other hand, he has absolutely nothing ... On the other hand,
things can not get worse for him, they can only get
better ...

             (Sings)

                          45

TEVYE (Continued)
THEY GAVE EACH OTHER A PLEDGE.
UNHEARD OF, ABSURD.
THEY GAVE EACH OTHER A PLEDGE.
UNTHINKABLE.
BUT LOOK AT MY DAUGHTER'S FACE,
SHE LOVES HIM, SHE WANTS HIM
AND LOOK AT MY DAUGHTER'S EYES,
SO HOPEFUL.

        (Spoken)
Tradition. Aaah!
        (To audience)
Well, children, when shall we make the wedding?

                    TZEITEL
Thank you, Papa.

                    MOTEL
Reb Tevye, you won't be sorry.

                    TEVYE
I won't be sorry? I'm sorry already.

                    TZEITEL
Thank you, Papa.

                    MOTEL
Thank you, Papa.

                    TEVYE
Thank you, Papa ... They pledged their troth ...
        (Starts exit L, then looks
        back at them)
Modern children ... Golde! What will I tell Golde? What am
I going to do about Golde?
        (To Heaven)
Help!
        (Exit L)

                    TZEITEL
Motel, you were wonderful!

                    MOTEL
It was a miracle! It was a miracle.

        (Sings)
WONDER OF WONDERS, MIRACLE OF MIRACLES
GOD TOOK A DANIEL ONCE AGAIN
STOOD BY HIS SIDE, AND MIRACLE OF MIRACLES
WALKED HIM THROUGH THE LION'S DEN.

WONDER OF WONDERS, MIRACLE OF MIRACLES
I WAS AFRAID THAT GOD WOULD FROWN
BUT LIKE HE DID SO LONG AGO IN JERICHO
GOD JUST MADE A WALL FALL DOWN.

WHEN MOSES SOFTENED PHAROAH'S HEART
THAT WAS A MIRACLE
WHEN GOD MADE THE WATERS OF THE RED SEA PART
THAT WAS A MIRACLE, TOO.

BUT OF ALL GOD'S MIRACLES LARGE AND SMALL
THE MOST MIRACULOUS ONE OF ALL
IS THAT OUT OF A WORTHLESS LUMP OF CLAY
GOD HAS MADE A MAN TODAY.

WONDER OF WONDERS, MIRACLE OF MIRACLES
GOD TOOK A TAILOR BY THE HAND
TURNED HIM AROUND, AND MIRACLE OF MIRACLES
LED HIM TO THE PROMISED LAND

WHEN DAVID SLEW GOLIATH, YES!
THAT WAS A MIRACLE
WHEN GOD GAVE US MANNA IN THE WILDERNESS
THAT WAS A MIRACLE, TOO.

BUT OF ALL GOD'S MIRACLES LARGE AND SMALL
THE MOST MIRACULOUS ONE OF ALL
IS THE ONE I THOUGHT COULD NEVER BE
GOD HAS GIVEN YOU TO ME.

DIMOUT

ACT I

Scene 7

                        TEVYE's bedroom.

         AT RISE: It is in complete darkness. In the
                        dark, we hear a groan ... then
                        another ... then a scream ...

                        TEVYE
Aagh ... Lazar ... Motel ... Tzeitel ...

                        GOLDE'S VOICE
What is it? What?

                        TEVYE'S VOICE
Help! Help! Help!

                        GOLDE'S VOICE
Tevye, wake up!

              (Lights slowly go up, as GOLDE
              lights the lamp ... revealing the
              bedroom. TEVYE and GOLDE are in
              separate beds; TEVYE, still asleep,
              yells "Help, help")

                        GOLDE
              (Continues, shaking him)
Tevye! What's the matter with you? Why are you howling
like that?

                        TEVYE
              (Opens his eyes, frightened)
Where is she? Where is she?

                        GOLDE
Where is who? What are you talking about?

                        TEVYE
Fruma-Sarah. Lazar Wolf's first wife, Fruma-Sarah. She
was standing here a minute ago.

                        GOLDE
What's the matter with you, Tevye? Fruma-Sarah has been
dead for years. You must have been dreaming. Tell me what
you dreamt, and I'll tell you what it meant.

                        TEVYE
It was terrible.

                          GOLDE
Tell me.

                          TEVYE
All right -- only don't be frightened.

                          GOLDE
               (Impatiently)
Tell me!

                          TEVYE
All right, this was my dream. In the beginning I dreamt
that we were having a celebration of some kind. Everybody
we knew was there ... and musicians too ...

               (As HE speaks, MEN, WOMEN, MUSICIANS
               start to enter the bedroom ... TEVYE,
               wearing a nightgown, starts to get
               out of bed to join the dream ...)
In the middle of the dream, in walks your grandmother
Tzeitel, may she rest in peace.

                          GOLDE
               (Alarmed)
Grandmother Tzeitel? How did she look?

                          TEVYE
For a woman who is dead thirty years, she looked very good.
Naturally, I went up to greet her ... She said to me ...

               (GRANDMA TZEITEL now enters the
               dream, and TEVYE approaches her,
               greets her in pantomime ... The
               music has started, under, and
               GRANDMA starts to sing ...)

          SONG: "THE DREAM"

                          GRANDMA
          A BLESSING ON YOUR HEAD,

                          RABBI
          MAZELTOV, MAZELTOV

                          GRANDMA
          TO SEE A DAUGHTER WED

                          RABBI
          MAZELTOV, MAZELTOV

                          GRANDMA
          AND SUCH A SON-IN-LAW
          LIKE NO ONE EVER SAW
          THE TAILOR MOTEL KAMZOIL

                            49

                              GOLDE
                    (Spoken, bewildered)
Motel?

                              GRANDMA
          A WORTHY BOY IS HE,

                              RABBI
          MAZELTOV, MAZELTOV

                              GRANDMA
          OF PIOUS FAMILY

                              RABBI
          MAZELTOV, MAZELTOV

                              GRANDMA
          THEY NAMED HIM AFTER MY
          DEAR UNCLE MORDECAI
          THE TAILOR MOTEL KAMZOIL.

                              GOLDE
                    (Spoken)
A tailor! She must have heard wrong. She meant a butcher.

                    (TEVYE has returned to GOLDE;
                    listens to this, then runs back
                    to GRANDMA)

                              TEVYE
          YOU MUST HAVE HEARD WRONG, GRANDMA
          THERE'S NO TAILOR
          YOU MEAN A BUTCHER, GRANDMA
          BY THE NAME OF LAZAR-WOLF

                              GRANDMA
          I MEAN TAILOR, TEVYE
          MY GREAT GRAN. ~~ILD
          MY LITTLE TZEITEL WHO YOU NAMED FOR ME
          MOTEL'S BRIDE WAS MEANT TO BE
          FOR SUCH A MATCH I PRAYED

                              CHORUS
          MAZELTOV, MAZELTOV

                              GRANDMA
          IN HEAVEN IT WAS MADE

                              CHORUS
          MAZELTOV, MAZELTOV

                              50

GRANDMA

A FINE UPSTANDING BOY
A COMFORT AND A JOY
THE TAILOR MOTEL KAMZOIL.

GOLDE
(From bed)
But we announced it already. We made a bargain with the
butcher.

TEVYE

BUT WE ANNOUNCED IT, GRANDMA
TO OUR NEIGHBORS
WE MADE A BARGAIN, GRANDMA
WITH THE BUTCHER, LAZAR WOLF

GRANDMA

SO YOU ANNOUNCED IT, TEVYE
THAT'S YOUR HEADACHE
BUT AS FOR LAZAR WOLF, I SAY TO YOU,
TEVYE, THAT'S YOUR HEADACHE TOO.

CHORUS

A BLESSING ON YOUR HOUSE, MAZELTOV, MAZELTOV
IMAGINE SUCH A SPOUSE, MAZELTOV, MAZELTOV
AND SUCH A SON-IN-LAW
LIKE NO ONE EVER SAW
THE TAILOR MOTEL KAMZOIL.

THE TAILOR MOTEL KAMZOIL

TEVYE

THE TAILOR MOTEL KAM ...

CHORUS

SHAH! SHAH!
LOOK!

WHO IS THIS?
WHO IS THIS?
WHO COMES HERE?
WHO? WHO? WHO? WHO?
WHAT WOMAN IS THIS
BY RIGHTEOUS ANGER SHAKEN?

SOLO VOICES

COULD IT BE?
SURE?
YES IT COULD?
WHY NOT?
WHO COULD BE MISTAKEN?

CHORUS

IT'S THE BUTCHER'S WIFE COME FROM BEYOND THE GRAVE
IT'S THE BUTCHER'S DEAR DARLING DEPARTED WIFE
FRUMA-SARAH, FRUMA-SARAH
FRUMA-SARAH, FRUMA-SARAH, FRUMA-SARAH, etc.

FRUMA-SARAH

TEVYE! TEVYE!
WHAT IS THIS ABOUT YOUR DAUGHTER MARRYING MY HUSBAND?

CHORUS

YES, HER HUSBAND.

FRUMA-SARAH

WOULD YOU DO THIS TO YOUR FRIEND AND NEIGHBOR,
    FRUMA-SARAH

CHORUS

FRUMA-SARAH

FRUMA-SARAH

HAVE YOU NO CONSIDERATION FOR A WOMAN'S FEELINGS

CHORUS

WOMAN'S FEELINGS?

FRUMA-SARAH

HANDING OVER MY BELONGINGS TO A TOTAL STRANGER.

CHORUS

TOTAL STRANGER.

FRUMA-SARAH

HOW CAN YOU ALLOW IT, HOW?
HOW CAN YOU LET YOUR DAUGHTER TAKE MY PLACE?
LIVE IN MY HOUSE ... CARRY MY KEYS
AND WEAR MY CLOTHES ... PEARLS ... HOW?

CHORUS

HOW CAN YOU ALLOW YOUR DAUGHTER
TO TAKE HER PLACE ...

FRUMA-SARAH

PEARLS ...

CHORUS

HOUSE ... KEYS ... CLOTHES ... HOW?

FRUMA-SARAH

TEVYE!!

CHORUS

TEVYE!

                         FRUMA-SARAH
SUCH A LEARNED MAN AS TEVYE WOULDN'T LET IT HAPPEN

                    CHORUS
LET IT HAPPEN

                         FRUMA-SARAH
TELL ME THAT IT ISN'T TRUE AND THEN I WOULDN'T WORRY

                    CHORUS
WOULDN'T WORRY

                         FRUMA-SARAH
SAY YOU DIDN'T GIVE YOUR BLESSING TO YOUR DAUGHTER'S
     MARRIAGE

                    CHORUS
DAUGHTER'S MARRIAGE

                    FRUMA-SARAH
LET ME TELL YOU WHAT WOULD FOLLOW SUCH A FATAL WEDDING.

                    CHORUS
FATAL WEDDING.
-- SHH!!

                         FRUMA-SARAH
IF TZEITEL MARRIES LAZAR WOLF
I PITY THEM BOTH
SHE'LL LIVE WITH HIM THREE WEEKS
AND WHEN THREE WEEKS ARE UP
I'LL COME TO HER BY NIGHT
I'LL TAKE HER BY THE THROAT
AND ...
THIS I'LL GIVE YOU TZEITEL
THIS I'LL GIVE YOU TZEITEL
THAT I'LL GIVE YOU TZEITEL
HERE'S MY WEDDING PRESENT IF SHE MARRIES LAZAR WOLF!
     (SHE starts choking TEVYE)

                    GOLDE
          (While TEVYE is being choked)
It's an evil spirit! May it fall into the river; may it
sink into the earth. Such a dark and horrible dream! And
to think it was brought on by that butcher. If my
grandmother Tzeitel, may she rest in peace, took the
trouble to come all the way from the other world to tell
us about the tailor, all we can say is that it is all for
the best, and it couldn't possibly be any better. Amen.

                    TEVYE
Amen.

          (CHORUS exits during this speech
          ... GOLDE sings ...)

                    GOLDE
A BLESSING ON MY HEAD, MAZELTOV, MAZELTOV
LIKE GRANDMA TZEITEL SAID, MAZELTOV, MAZELTOV
WE'LL HAVE A SON-IN-LAW
LIKE NO ONE EVER SAW
THE TAILOR MOTEL KAMZOIL.

                    TEVYE
WE HAVEN'T GOT THE MAN,

                    GOLDE
MAZELTOV, MAZELTOV

                    TEVYE
WE HAD WHEN WE BEGAN,

                    GOLDE
MAZELTOV, MAZELTOV

                    TEVYE
BUT SINCE YOUR GRANDMA CAME
SHE'LL MARRY WHAT'S HIS NAME?

                    GOLDE
THE TAILOR MOTEL KAMZOIL

                    BOTH
THE TAILOR MOTEL KAMZOIL,
THE TAILOR MOTEL KAMZOIL,
THE TAILOR MOTEL KAMZOIL.

            SLOW BLACKOUT

54

Village street and MOTEL's Tailor
Shop

                    JOHN
Bagels, fresh bagels.

                    WOMAN
Did you hear? Did you hear? Tevye's Tzeitel is marrying
Motel, not Lazar Wolf.

                    ALL
No.

                    WOMAN
Yes.

                    MENDEL
Tzeitel is marrying Motel?

                    WOMAN
Yes!

                    ALL
          (Outside)
No!

                    ALL
          (Inside)
Mazeltov, Motel.

          (THEY rush into the tailor shop,
          surround MOTEL, shouting Mazeltov,
          Congratulations, etc.)

                    INNKEEPER
What's all the excitement?

                    AVRAM
Tevye's Tzeitel going to marry ...

                    INNKEEPER
I know, Lazar Wolf, the butcher.

                    GROUP
No!

                    AVRAM
No, Motel, the Tailor.

                    INNKEEPER
Motel, the tailor, that's terrible!
        (Rushes into shop)
Mazeltov, Motel.

                    WOMAN
        (To SHANDEL, exiting from shop)
Imagine! Tzeitel is marrying Motel. I can't believe it!

                    SHANDEL
What's wrong with my son, Motel?

                    WOMAN
Oh, excuse me, Shandel. Mazeltov.

                    ALL
        (Inside shop)
Mazeltov, mazeltov, etc.

                    MOTEL
Yussel, do you have a wedding hat for me?

                    YUSSEL
Lazar Wolf ordered a hat but it's not cheap.

                    MOTEL
I got his bride, I can get his hat!

                    YUSSEL
Then come, Motel, come.

                    MOTEL
Chava, can you watch the shop for a few minutes? I'll be
back soon.

                    CHAVA
Of course.

                    MOTEL
Thank you, Chava.

        (ALL exit from shop, calling
        Mazeltovs. INNKEEPER rushes out
        as LAZAR crosses)

                    YUSSEL
Come, Motel. I'll show you.

                    ALL
We just heard about your sister ... Mazeltov, Chava ...
Mazeltov, Chava.

                              CHAVA
Thank ... thank you very much ...

                    (FYEDKA and two other RUSSIANS
                    enter at the same time. As OTHERS
                    exit, THEY cross to CHAVA, blocking
                    her way into the shop)

                              RUSSIANS
                    (Mockingly, imitating others,
                     slight mispronunciation)
Mazeltov, Chava ... Mazeltov, Chava ...

                              CHAVA
Please may I pass.

                              SASHA
Why? We're congratulating you ...

                              RUSSIANS
Mazeltov, Chava.

                              FYEDKA
                    (Calmly)
All right, stop it!

                              SASHA
What's wrong with you?

                              FYEDKA
Just stop it.

                              SASHA
Now listen here, Fyedka ...

                              FYEDKA
Goodbye, Sasha ...

                    (THEY hesitate)

I said goodbye!

                    (THEY look at FYEDKA curiously,
                    then exit)

I'm sorry about that. They mean no harm.

                              CHAVA
Don't they?
                    (SHE enters shop. HE follows
                    her in)
Is there something you want?

                              FYEDKA
Yes. I'd like to talk to you.

                               57

                              CHAVA
I'd rather not.
          (SHE hesitates)

                              FYEDKA
I've often noticed you at the bookseller's. Not many girls
in this village like to read ...
          (Sudden thought ... extends book
          HE is holding)
Would you like to borrow this book? It's very good.

                              CHAVA
No, thank you.

                              FYEDKA
Why. Because I'm not Jewish? Do you feel about us the way
they feel about you? I didn't think you would ...

                              CHAVA
What do you know about me?

                              FYEDKA
Let me tell you about myself. I'm a pleasant fellow,
charming, honest, ambitious, quite bright, and very modest.

                              CHAVA
I don't think we should be talking this way.

                              FYEDKA
I often do things I shouldn't ... Go ahead, take the book ...
It's by Heinrich Heine. Happens to be Jewish, I believe.

                              CHAVA
That doesn't matter.

                              FYEDKA
You're quite right. Good. After you return it, I'll ask
you how you like it, and we'll talk about it for awhile,
then we'll talk about Life, how we feel about things, and
it can all turn out quite pleasant.

          (MOTEL enters)

                              MOTEL
Oh, Fyedka! -- Can I do something for you?

                              FYEDKA
No, thank you.
          (Starts out)

                              MOTEL
Oh, you forgot your book.

                         CHAVA
No, it's mine.

                         MOTEL
Thank you, Chava.

          (CHAVA takes book, exits)

                         FYEDKA
Good day, Chava.

                         CHAVA   SET:
. Good day.

                         FYEDKA
          (Pleasantly)
Fyedka.

                         CHAVA
Good day, Fyedka.

          (THEY exit ... MOTEL puts on
          his wedding hat)

ACT   I

Scene   9

MUSICIANS lead us to:

SET:

Section of TEVYE's yard. Night.
TZEITEL, in bridal gown, enter,
followed by her PARENTS, SISTERS,
OTHERS. MOTEL enters, followed by
his PARENTS, OTHERS. MANY GUESTS
enter carrying lit candles. The
MEN take their places at right, as
a group; the WOMEN at left, TZEITEL
and MOTEL in center.

MOTEL places a veil over TZEITEL's
head.

FOUR MEN enter, carrying canopy.
THEY are followed by the RABBI.
The canopy is placed over the heads
of MOTEL and TZEITEL.

GUESTS start singing: "SUNRISE,
SUNSET." Song is sustained through
following:

RABBI lifts TZEITEL's veil. HE
pantomimes prayer over goblet of
wine, hands it to BRIDE and GROOM,
and THEY each sip.

TZEITEL then slowly walks in a
circle around MOTEL.

MOTEL places ring on TZEITEL's
finger,

RABBI places a wine glass on the
floor,

SONG ends. A moment's pause.

MOTEL treads on glass.

At the moment the glass breaks,
ALL shout "Mazel Tov."

OPEN TO: Full yard. It is divid-
ed partly down the center by a
short partition; several tables are
set up in rear of each section.

60

                    GOLDE
IS THIS THE LITTLE GIRL I CARRIED
IS THIS THE LITTLE BOY AT PLAY

                    TEVYE
I DON'T REMEMBER GROWING OLDER

                    GOLDE
WHEN DID THEY?
WHEN DID SHE GET TO BE A BEAUTY?
WHEN DID HE GET TO BE SO TALL?

                    TEVYE
WASN'T IT YESTERDAY WHEN THEY WERE SMALL?

                    BOYS
SUNRISE, SUNSET
SUNRISE, SUNSET
SWIFTLY FLOW THE DAYS
SEEDLINGS TURN OVERNIGHT TO SUNFLOWERS
BLOSSOMING EVEN AS WE GAZE

                    GIRLS
SUNRISE, SUNSET
SUNRISE, SUNSET
SWIFTLY FLY THE YEARS
ONE SEASON FOLLOWING ANOTHER
LADEN WITH HAPPINESS AND TEARS.

                    GOLDE
WHAT WORDS OF WISDOM CAN I GIVE THEM?
HOW CAN I HELP TO EASE THEIR WAY?

                    TEVYE
NOW THEY MUST LEARN FROM ONE ANOTHER
DAY BY DAY.

                    PERCHIK
THEY LOOK SO NATURAL TOGETHER

                    HODEL
JUST LIKE TWO NEWLYWEDS SHOULD BE

                    PERCHIK/HODEL
IS THERE A CANOPY IN STORE FOR ME?

                    GIRLS and BOYS
SUNRISE, SUNSET
SUNRISE, SUNSET
SWIFTLY FLY THE YEARS
ONE SEASON FOLLOWING ANOTHER
LADEN WITH HAPPINESS AND TEARS.

        (MOTEL breaks glass)

                    ALL
MAZELTOV!

ACT   I

Scene 10

Yard of TEVYE's house. After the
dance, all seat themselves on
benches at tables pulled up on
either side of the partition. WOMEN
are on the left, MEN on the right.

As the dance concludes, INNKEEPER
mounts a stool and signals for
silence. The noise subsides.

ALL

Shah...shah ... quiet ... Reb Mordcha ... shah ... shah.

INNKEEPER

My friends, we are gathered here to share the joy of the
newlyweds, Motel and Tzeitel, may they live together in
peace to a ripe old age, amen ...

ALL

Amen.

(RABBI slowly makes his way to the
table, assisted by MENDEL)

INNKEEPER

Ah, here comes our beloved rabbi. May he be with us for
many, many years.

RABBI

Amen.

ALL

Amen.

INNKEEPER

I want to announce, that the bride's parents are giving the
newlyweds the following: a new featherbed ... a pair of
goose pillows.

GOLDE
(Shouts from women's side)

Goose pillows ...

INNKEEPER

Goose pillows. And this pair of candlesticks ...

62

                              ALL
Mazeltov!

                           INNKEEPER
Now let us not in our joy tonight forget those who are no
longer with us, our dear departed, who lived in pain and
poverty and hardship and who died in pain and poverty and
hardship.

          (There are sobs from the GROUP)

But enough tears.

          (GROUP stops its mourning immediately)

Let's be merry and content, like our good friend, Lazar Wolf,
who has everything in the world, except a bride.

          (Laughter)

But Lazar has no ill feelings. In fact, he has a gift for
the newlyweds that he wants to announce himself. Come,
Lazar Wolf.

                            LAZAR
          (Rises)
Like he said, I have no ill feelings. What's done is done ...
I am giving the newlyweds, five chickens, one for each of
the first five Sabbaths of their wedded life.

          (Murmurs of appreciation. TEVYE
          rises to accept)

                            TEVYE
Reb Lazar, you are a decent man. In the name of my
daughter and her new husband, I accept your gift. There
is a famous saying that ...

                            LAZAR
Reb Tevye, I'm not marrying your daughter. I don't have
to listen to your sayings.

                            TEVYE
If you would listen a second, I was only going to say ...

                            LAZAR
Why should I listen to you? A man who breaks an agreement!

          (Murmurs from GROUP)

                            MENDEL
Not now, Lazar, in the middle of a wedding.

                    LAZAR
I have a right to talk.

                    TEVYE
          (Angry)
What right? This is not your wedding.

                    LAZAR
It should have been!

          (ALL react - murmurs)

                    MENDEL
Reb Lazar, don't shame Reb Tevye at his daughter's wedding.

                    LAZAR
But he shamed me in front of the whole village!

          (Bedlam begins, EVERYONE takes
          sides)

That's true ... the Rabbi said ... it was a shame ... he has
no feelings ... this is not the place ..

                    MENDEL
Shah ... shah ... quiet, the Rabbi. The Rabbi, the Rabbi.
Rabbi, say something.

                    RABBI
          (Rises, as noise subsides)
I say ... I say ... Let's sit down.
          (Sits)

                    TEVYE
We all heard the wise words of the Rabbi.

          (ALL return to their seats)

                    INNKEEPER
Now, I'd like to sing a little song that ...

                    TEVYE
          (Bursts out)
You can keep your diseased chickens.

                    LAZAR
Leave my chickens out of this. We made a bargain.

                    TEVYE
The terms weren't settled.

                    LAZAR
We drank on it ...

                              MAN (Lou)
I saw them, they drank on it ...

                              2nd MAN (Mitch)
But the terms weren't settled ...

                              SHANDEL
What's done is done ...

                              TEVYE
Once a butcher always a butcher ...

                              GOLDE
I had a sign. My own grandmother came to us from the
grave ..

                              YENTE
What sign? What grandmother? My grandfather came to me
from the grave and told me that her grandmother was a big
liar.

                              LAZAR
We drank on it.

              (Bedlam. INNKEEPER tries to quiet
              them. PERCHIK climbs onto a stool,
              banging two tin plates together)

                              INNKEEPER
Quiet, I'm singing ...

                              TEVYE
The terms weren't settled ..

                              GOLDE
I had a sign ...

                              YENTE
An agreement is an agreement ...

                              PERCHIK
Quiet! Quiet! What's all the screaming about? "They
drank on it .. and agreement ... a sign." ... It's all
nonsense. Tzeitel wanted to marry Motel and not Lazar.

                              MENDEL
A young girl decides for herself?

                              PERCHIK
Why not? Yes! They love each other.

                              AVRAM
Love!

                        LAZAR
Terrible!

                        MENDEL
He's a radical!

                        YENTE
What happens to the matchmaker?

            (ALL react violently, joining
            in the argument)

                        RABBI
I say ... I say ...

                        TEVYE
I know -- Let's sit down.

                        INNKEEPER
Musicians, play ... a dance, a dance ...

            (Music starts, but no one dances)
Come on, dance ... It's a wedding.

                        YENTE
Some wedding!

            (PERCHIK crosses to women's side)

                        AVRAM
What's he doing?

                        TEVYE
Perchik!

                        MAN (Lou)
Stop him!

                        PERCHIK
            (To HODEL)
Who will dance with me?

                        MENDEL
That's a sin!

                        PERCHIK
It's no sin to dance at a wedding.

                        AVRAM
But with a girl?

66

                              LAZAR
That's what comes from bringing a wild man into your house.

                              TEVYE
He's not a wild man. His ideas are a little different,
but ...

                              MENDEL
It's a sin.

                              PERCHIK
It's no sin. Ask the Rabbi. Ask him.

          (ALL gather around RABBI)

                              TEVYE
Well, Rabbi?

                              RABBI
Dancing ... Well, it's not exactly forbidden, but ...

                              TEVYE
There, you see? It's not forbidden.

                              PERCHIK
And it's no sin. Now will someone dance with me?

          (HODEL rises to dance)

                              GOLDE
Hodel!

                              HODEL
It's only a dance, mama.

                              PERCHIK
Play!

                              LAZAR
Look at Tevye's daughter.

                              MENDEL
She's dancing with a man.

                              TEVYE
I can see she's dancing ... And I'm going to dance with my
wife. Golde.

                              SHANDEL
Golde!

          (As MOTEL crosses to TZEITEL)

Motel!

                               67

(THEY ALL dance, except for LAZAR
and YENTE, who storm off. As the
dance reaches a wild high point,
the CONSTABLE and his MEN enter)

                    CONSTABLE
I see we came at a bad time, Tevye. I'm sorry, but the
orders are for tonight. For the whole village ...

          (To MUSICIANS)

Go on, play. Play ... All right, men.

                    (The RUSSIANS begin their destruction,
                    turning over tables, throwing pillows,
                    smashing dishes and the window of the
                    house. ONE of them throws the
                    wedding-gift candlesticks to the
                    ground, and PERCHIK grapples with
                    him. But HE is hit with a club and
                    falls to the ground)

                    HODEL
No, Perchik!

                    (During this ALL the GUESTS have
                    left ... The MUSICIANS remain)

                    CONSTABLE
          (To his MEN)
All right, enough!
          (To TEVYE)
I am genuinely sorry. You understand.

                    TEVYE
          (Mock courtesy)
Of course.

                    CONSTABLE
          (To his MEN)
Come.

          (THEY exit)

                    GOLDE
Take him in the house.

                    TEVYE
What are you standing around for? Clean up. Clean up.

(THEY start straightening up,
pick up broken dishes, bring bedding
back to house. TZEITEL picks up
candlesticks, one of which is broken.
SEVERAL PEOPLE, including FYEDKA, are
at fence of yard, looking on. CHAVA
looks up, notices him, continues
cleaning up ...

TEVYE starts to enter house.
MUSICIANS remain ...)

CURTAIN

ACT II

Prologue

TEVYE

That was quite a dowry you gave my daughter Tzeitel at her
wedding. Was that necessary?

... Anyway, Tzeitel and Motel have been married almost two
months now. They work very hard, they are as poor as
synagogue mice. ... But they are both so happy they don't
know how miserable they are. Motel keeps talking about a
sewing machine. I know you're very busy, God, -- wars and
revolutions, floods, plagues -- all those little things
that bring people to You -- couldn't You take a second away
from your catastrophes and get it for him? How much
trouble would it be? ... Oh, and while You're in the
neighborhood, my horse's left leg ... Am I bothering You
too much? ... I'm sorry. As the good book says ... Why
should I tell you what the good book says?

ACT II

Scene 1

Exterior of TEVYE's house. HODEL
enters, petulantly, followed by
PERCHIK.

PERCHIK
Please don't be upset, Hodel.

HODEL
Why should I be upset? If you must leave, you must.

PERCHIK
I do have to. They expect me in Kiev tomorrow morning.

HODEL
So you told me. Then goodbye.

PERCHIK
Great changes are about to take place in this country.
Tremendous changes. But they can't happen by themselves ...

HODEL
So naturally you feel that you personally have to ...

PERCHIK
Not only me. Many people. Jews, Gentiles, many people hate
what is going on. Don't you understand?

HODEL
I understand, of course. You want to leave. Then goodbye.

PERCHIK
Hodel, your father, the others here, think what happened at
Tzeitel's wedding was a little cloudburst and it's over and
everything will now be peaceful again. It won't. ...
Horrible things are happening all over the land ... pogroms,
violence, whole villages are being emptied of their people.
... and it's reaching everywhere, and it will reach here.
You understand?

HODEL
Yes, I ... I suppose I do.

PERCHIK
I have work to do. The greatest work a man can do.

HODEL
Then goodbye, Perchik.

71

                    PERCHIK
Before I go,
          (HE hesitates, summons up courage)
there is a certain question I wish to discuss with you.

                    HODEL
Yes?

                    PERCHIK
A political question.

                    HODEL
What is it?

                    PERCHIK
The question of marriage.

                    HODEL
This is a political question?

                    PERCHIK
In a theoretical sense, yes. The relationship between a
man and woman known as marriage is based on mutual beliefs,
a common attitude and philosophy towards society ...

                    HODEL
And affection ...

                    PERCHIK
And affection ... This relationship has positive social
values. It reflects a unity and solidarity ...

                    HODEL
And affection ...

                    PERCHIK
Yes, and I personally am in favor of it. Do you understand?

                    HODEL
Yes. I think you are asking me to marry you.

                    PERCHIK
In a theoretical sense, yes, I am.

                    HODEL
I was hoping you were.

                    PERCHIK
Then I take it you approve. And we can consider ourselves
engaged, even though I am going away?

          (SHE nods)

I am very happy, Hodel. Very happy.

                         72

                    HODEL
So am I, Perchik.   What's the matter?

                    PERCHIK
        (Sings)
    I USED TO TELL MYSELF
    THAT I HAD EVERYTHING
    BUT THAT WAS ONLY HALF TRUE.
    I HAD AN AIM IN LIFE
    AND THAT WAS EVERYTHING
    BUT NOW I EVEN HAVE YOU.

    I HAVE SOMETHING THAT I WOULD DIE FOR
    SOMEONE THAT I CAN LIVE FOR,TOO.

    YES, NOW I HAVE EVERYTHING
    NOT ONLY EVERYTHING
    I HAVE A LITTLE BIT MORE
    BESIDES HAVING EVERYTHING
    I KNOW WHAT EVERYTHING'S FOR.

    I USED TO WONDER
    COULD THERE BE A WIFE
    TO SHARE SUCH A DIFFICULT, WAND'RING KIND OF LIFE?

                    HODEL
    I WAS ONLY OUT OF SIGHT
    WAITING RIGHT HERE

                    PERCHIK
    WHO KNOWS TOMORROW
    WHERE OUR HOME WILL BE

                    HODEL
    I'LL BE WITH YOU AND THAT'S
    HOME ENOUGH FOR ME

                    PERCHIK
    EVERYTHING IS RIGHT AT HAND

                    BOTH
    SIMPLE AND CLEAR

                    PERCHIK
    I HAVE SOMETHING THAT I WOULD DIE FOR
    SOMEONE THAT I COULD LIVE FOR, TOO

    YES, NOW I HAVE EVERYTHING
    NOT ONLY EVERYTHING
    I HAVE A LITTLE BIT MORE
    BESIDES HAVING EVERYTHING
    I KNOW WHAT EVERYTHING'S FOR.

                    HODEL
And when will we be married, Perchik?

                    PERCHIK
I will send for you as soon as I can. It will be a hard
life, Hodel.

                    HODEL
But it will be less hard ... if we live it together.

                    PERCHIK
Yes.

                    TEVYE
          (Entering)
Good evening.

                    PERCHIK
Good evening, Reb Tevye, I have some bad news. I must leave
this place.

                    TEVYE
When?

                    PERCHIK
Right away.

                    TEVYE
I'm sorry, Perchik. We will all miss you.

                    PERCHIK
But I also have some good news. You can congratulate me.

                    TEVYE
Congratulations. What for?

                    PERCHIK
We're engaged.

                    TEVYE
Engaged?

                    HODEL
Yes, Papa, we're engaged.

                    TEVYE
No, you're not. I know, you like him, and he likes you,
but you're going away, and you're staying here, so have a
nice trip, Perchik. I hope you'll be very happy, and my
answer is no.

                    HODEL
Please, Papa, you don't understand.

                    TEVYE
I understand. I gave my permission to Motel and Tzeitel,
so you feel that you also have a right. I'm sorry, Perchik.
I like you, but you're going away, so go in good health and
my answer is still no.

                    HODEL
You don't understand, Papa.

                    TEVYE
You're not listening. I say no. I'm sorry, Hodel, but
we'll find someone else for you, here in Anatevka.

                    PERCHIK
Reb Tevye.

                    TEVYE
What is it?

                    PERCHIK
We are not asking for your permission, only for your
blessing. We are going to get married.

                    TEVYE
          (To HODEL)
You're not asking for my permission?

                    HODEL
But we would like your blessing, Papa.

                    TEVYE
          I CAN'T BELIEVE MY OWN EARS. MY BLESSING? FOR WHAT?
          FOR GOING OVER MY HEAD? IMPOSSIBLE.
          AT LEAST WITH TZEITEL AND MOTEL, THEY ASKED ME,
          THEY BEGGED ME.
          BUT NOW IF I LIKE IT OR NOT
          YOU'LL MARRY HIM.
          SO WHAT DO YOU WANT FROM ME? GO ON, BE WED.
          AND TEAR OUT MY BEARD AND UNCOVER MY HEAD
          TRADITION
          THEY'RE NOT EVEN ASKING PERMISSION
          FROM THE PAPA
          WHAT'S HAPPENING TO THE TRADITION?
          ONE LITTLE TIME I PULLED OUT A THREAD
          AND WHERE HAS IT LED? WHERE HAS IT LED?

Where has it led? To this! A man tells me he is getting
married. He doesn't ask me, he tells me. But first, he
abandons her.

                    HODEL
He is not abandoning me, Papa.

                       75

PERCHIK

As soon as I can, I will send for her and marry her. I love
her.

TEVYE

He loves her. Love. It's a new style. On the other hand,
our old ways were once new, weren't they? On the other hand,
they decided without parents, without a matchmaker. After
all, did Adam and Eve have a matchmaker? ... Yes, they did.
... Then it seems these two have the same matchmaker.

    THEY'RE GOING OVER MY HEAD
    UNHEARD OF ... ABSURD
    FOR THIS THEY WANT TO BE BLESSED
    UNTHINKABLE.

    I'LL LOCK HER UP IN HER ROOM
    I COULDN'T ... I SHOULD
    BUT LOOK AT MY DAUGHTER'S EYES
    SHE LOVES HIM

    TRADITION ...

        (To them)
Very well, children, you have my blessing and my permission.

HODEL

Oh, thank you, Papa. You don't know how happy that makes
me.

TEVYE

What else could I do?

PERCHIK

Thank you, Papa.

TEVYE

Thank you, Papa. ... What will I tell your mother? ...
Another dream?

PERCHIK

Perhaps if you tell her something ... that I am going to
visit a rich uncle, something like that.

TEVYE

Please, Perchik. I can handle my own wife.

        (THEY exit)

Golde! ... Golde!
        (Timidly)
Hello, Golde. ... I've just been talking to Perchik and
Hodel.

                    GOLDE

Well?

                    TEVYE

They seem to be very fond of each other ...

                    GOLDE

Well?

                    TEVYE

I have decided to give them my permission to become engaged.
... I have to go inside and ...

                    GOLDE

What? Just like this? Without even asking me?

                    TEVYE

          (Roars)
Who asks you? I'm the father.

                    GOLDE

Who is he? A pauper. He has nothing, absolutely nothing!

                    TEVYE

          (Hesitates)
I wouldn't say that. I hear he has a rich uncle ... a very
rich uncle.
          (Changes subject)
He is a good man, Golde. I like him. He is a little crazy
but I like him. And what's more important, Hodel likes him.
Hodel loves him. So what can we do? It's a new world ...
a new world. Love. Golde ...
          (Sings)
     DO YOU LOVE ME?

                    GOLDE

     DO I WHAT?

                    TEVYE

     DO YOU LOVE ME?

                    GOLDE

     DO I LOVE YOU?
          WITH OUR DAUGHTERS GETTING MARRIED
          AND THIS TROUBLE IN THE TOWN
          YOU'RE UPSET, YOU'RE WORN OUT
          GO INSIDE, GO LIE DOWN
          MAYBE IT'S INDIGESTION

                    TEVYE

Golde, I'm asking you a question ...
     DO YOU LOVE ME?

                    GOLDE
     YOU'RE A FOOL.

                    TEVYE
I know ...
     BUT DO YOU LOVE ME?

                    GOLDE
     DO I LOVE YOU?
          FOR TWENTY-FIVE YEARS I'VE WASHED YOUR CLOTHES
          COOKED YOUR MEALS, CLEANED YOUR HOUSE
          GIVEN YOU CHILDREN, MILKED THE COW
          AFTER TWENTY-FIVE YEARS, WHY TALK ABOUT
               LOVE RIGHT NOW?

                    TEVYE
     GOLDE, THE FIRST TIME I MET YOU
     WAS ON OUR WEDDING DAY
     I WAS SCARED

                    GOLDE
     I WAS SHY.

                    TEVYE
     I WAS NERVOUS

                    GOLDE
     SO WAS I.

                    TEVYE
     BUT MY FATHER AND MY MOTHER
     SAID WE'D LEARN TO LOVE EACH OTHER
     AND NOW I'M ASKING, GOLDE
     DO YOU LOVE ME?

                    GOLDE
     I'M YOUR WIFE.

                    TEVYE
I know ...
     BUT DO YOU LOVE ME?

                    GOLDE
     DO I LOVE HIM?
          FOR TWENTY-FIVE YEARS I'VE LIVED WITH HIM
          FOUGHT WITH HIM, STARVED WITH HIM
          TWENTY-FIVE YEARS MY BED IS HIS
          IF THAT'S NOT LOVE, WHAT IS?

                    TEVYE
     THEN YOU LOVE ME?

                    GOLDE
     I SUPPOSE I DO.

                    TEVYE
AND I SUPPOSE I LOVE YOU TOO.

                         BOTH
IT DOESN'T CHANGE A THING
BUT EVEN SO
AFTER TWENTY-FIVE YEARS,
IT'S NICE TO KNOW.

          <u>DIMOUT</u>

ACT II

Scene 2

Village street. YENTE, TZEITEL,
and OTHERS crossing. YENTE and
TZEITEL meet center stage.

LARRY

Fish -- Fresh fish!

YENTE

Oh, Tzeitel, Tzeitel darling. Guess who I just saw ... your
sister, Chava, with that Fyedka! And it's not the first
time I've seen them together.

TZEITEL

You saw Chava with Fyedka?

YENTE

Would I make it up? Oh, and Tzeitel, I happened to be at
the postoffice today and the postman told me there was a
letter there for your sister, Hodel.

TZEITEL

Wonderful, I'll go get it.

YENTE

I got it! It's from her intended, Perchik.
        (Hands letter to TZEITEL)

TZEITEL

Hodel will be so happy, she's been waiting ... But it's
open.

YENTE

It happened to be open ...

        (TZEITEL exits. YENTE watches her
        leave)

Rifka, I have such news for you.

    REMEMBER PERCHIK, THAT CRAZY STUDENT?
    REMEMBER AT THE WEDDING
    WHEN TZEITEL MARRIED MOTEL
    AND PERCHIK STARTED DANCING
    WITH TEVYE'S DAUGHTER HODEL?
    WELL, I JUST HEARD
    THAT PERCHIK'S BEEN ARRESTED, IN KIEV.

                              OTHERS
NO!

                              YENTE
YES!

                    (YENTE and GROUP exit R, WOMAN
                    (SUE) crosses to GROUP at L)

                         WOMAN (SUE)
Shandel, Shandel ... Wait till I tell you ...

          REMEMBER PERCHIK, THAT CRAZY STUDENT?
          REMEMBER AT THE WEDDING?
          HE DANCED WITH TEVYE'S HODEL
          WELL
          I JUST HEARD
          THAT HODEL'S BEEN ARRESTED, IN KIEV.

                         OTHERS
          NO. TERRIBLE, TERRIBLE.

                    (GROUP exits L, WOMAN (CAROL) crosses
                    to GROUP at R)

                         WOMAN (CAROL)
Mirala ...

          DO YOU REMEMBER PERCHIK
          THAT STUDENT, FROM KIEV?
          REMEMBER HOW HE ACTED
          WHEN TZEITEL MARRIED MOTEL?
          WELL, I JUST HEARD
          THAT MOTEL'S BEEN ARRESTED
          FOR DANCING AT THE WEDDING.

                              OTHERS
          NO!

                              WOMAN
          IN KIEV!

                    (GROUP exits R, MENDEL crosses to
                    GROUP at L)

                              MENDEL
Rabbi ... Rabbi ...

          REMEMBER PERCHIK, WITH ALL HIS STRANGE IDEAS?
          REMEMBER TZEITEL'S WEDDING?
          WHERE TEVYE DANCED WITH GOLDE
          WELL, I JUST HEARD
          THAT TEVYE'S BEEN ARRESTED
          AND GOLDE'S GONE TO KIEV.

                              81

                         GROUP
NO!

                         MENDEL
GOD FORBID.

                         GROUP
SHE DIDN'T.

                         MENDEL
SHE DID.

        (GROUP exits L. AVRAM crosses
        to GROUP R. YENTE enters from
        L, stands L edge of GROUP to
        listen)

                         AVRAM
Terrible news ... terrible ...

        REMEMBER PERCHIK
        WHO STARTED ALL THE TROUBLE
        WELL, I JUST HEARD FROM SOMEONE WHO SHOULD KNOW,
        THAT GOLDE'S BEEN ARRESTED
        AND HODEL'S GONE TO KIEV
        MOTEL STUDIES DANCING
        AND TEVYE'S ACTING STRANGE
        SHPRINTZE HAS THE MEASLES
        AND BIELKE HAS THE MUMPS.

                         YENTE
AND THAT'S WHAT COMES FROM MEN AND WOMEN DANCING!

              <u>BLACKOUT</u>

ACT II

Scene 3

Exterior of Railroad Station.
Morning. HODEL enters L, crosses
to bench. TEVYE follows, carrying
her suitcase.

                    HODEL
You don't have to wait for the train, Papa. You'll be late
for your customers.

                    TEVYE
Just a few more minutes. ... Is he in bad trouble, that hero
of yours?

          (SHE nods)

Arrested?

          (SHE nods)

And convicted?

                    HODEL
Yes, but he did nothing wrong. He cares nothing for himself,
everything he does is for humanity.

                    TEVYE
But if he did nothing wrong, he wouldn't be in trouble.

                    HODEL
Papa, how can you say that? What wrongs did Joseph do, and
Abraham, and Moses? And they had troubles.

                    TEVYE
... But why won't you tell me where he is now, this Joseph
of yours?

                    HODEL
It is far, Papa, terribly far ... He is in a settlement in
Siberia.

                    TEVYE
Siberia! And he asks you to leave your father and mother
and join him in that frozen wasteland, and marry him there?

                    HODEL
No, Papa, he did not ask me to go. I want to go. I don't
want him to be alone. I want to help him in his work. It
is the greatest work a man can do, Papa.

                              TEVYE
But, Hodel, baby ...

                              HODEL
Papa ...
          (Sings)
     HOW CAN I HOPE TO MAKE YOU UNDERSTAND
     WHY I DO ... WHAT I DO
     WHY I MUST TRAVEL TO A DISTANT LAND
     FAR FROM THE HOME I LOVE.

     ONCE I WAS HAPPILY CONTENT TO BE
     AS I WAS ... WHERE I WAS
     CLOSE TO THE PEOPLE WHO ARE CLOSE TO ME
     HERE IN THE HOME I LOVE.

     WHO COULD SEE THAT A MAN WOULD COME
     WHO WOULD CHANGE THE SHAPE OF MY DREAMS
     HELPLESS, NOW, I STAND WITH HIM
     WATCHING OLDER DREAMS GROW DIM.

     OH, WHAT A MELANCHOLY CHOICE THIS IS
     WANTING HOME, WANTING HIM
     CLOSING MY HEART TO EVERY HOPE BUT HIS
     LEAVING THE HOME I LOVE.

     THERE WHERE MY HEART HAS SETTLED LONG AGO
     I MUST GO ... I MUST GO
     WHO COULD IMAGINE I'D BE WAND'RING SO
     FAR FROM THE HOME I LOVE
     YET ... THERE WITH MY LOVE ... I'M HOME.

                              TEVYE
And who, my child, will there be to perform a marriage,
there in the wilderness?

                              HODEL
Papa, I promise you, we will be married under a canopy.

                              TEVYE
No doubt a rabbi or two was also arrested. ... Well, give
him my regards, this Moses of yours. I always thought he
was a good man. Tell him I rely on his honor to treat my
daughter well. Tell him that.

                              HODEL
Papa, God alone knows when we shall see each other again.

                              TEVYE
Then we will leave it in his hands.
               (HE kisses HODEL, starts off. HE
               stops, looks back, then looks to
               Heaven)

                               84

                    TEVYE (Continued)
Take care of her. See that she dresses warm.
           (HE exits. HODEL is seated on
           the station platform)

                 <u>DIMOUT</u>

ACT II

Scene 4

Village Street, some months later.
VILLAGERS enter.

AVRAM

Reb Mordcha, did you hear the news? A new arrival at Motel
and Tzeitel's.

INNKEEPER

A new arrival at Motel and Tzeitel's? I must congratulate
him.

AVRAM

Rabbi, did you hear the news? A new arrival at Motel and
Tzeitel's ...

RABBI

Really?

MENDEL

Mazeltov.

MAN (MITCH)

Mazeltov.

MAN (DAN)

Mazeltov.

(WOMAN and SHANDEL cross quickly)

WOMAN

Shandel, where are you running?

SHANDEL

To my boy, Motel. There's a new arrival there.

OTHERS

Mazeltov, Mazeltov, Mazeltov Shandel, etc.

(Open on Tailor Shop)

MOTEL's Tailor Shop. PEOPLE crowd
around MOTEL, congratulating him.

                    ALL
Mazeltov, Motel ... we just heard ... congratulations ...
wonderful, etc.

                    MOTEL
Thank you, thank you very much ...

          (TZEITEL enters)

                    AVRAM
Mazeltov, Tzeitel.

                    TZEITEL
You got it!

                    MOTEL
I got it!

                    TZEITEL
It's beautiful.

                    MOTEL
I know!

                    TZEITEL
Have you tried it yet?

                    MOTEL
          (Holds up two different-colored
          pieces of cloth sewn together)
Look.

                    TZEITEL
Beautiful.

                    MOTEL
I know. And in less than a minute. And see how close and
even the stitches are.

                    TZEITEL
Beautiful.

                    MOTEL
I know. From now on, my clothes will be perfect, made by
machine ... No more handmade clothes.

                    INNKEEPER
The Rabbi, the Rabbi.

                    MOTEL
Look, Rabbi, my new sewing machine.

                    RABBI
Mazeltov.

                    TZEITEL
Rabbi, is there a blessing for a sewing machine?

                    RABBI
There is a blessing for everything.
        (Prays)
Amen.

                    OTHERS
Amen. Mazeltov, etc.

        (ALL exit)

                    GOLDE
And the baby? How is the baby?

                    TZEITEL
He's wonderful, Mama.

            (FYEDKA enters. There is an
            awkward pause)

                    FYEDKA
Good afternoon.

                    MOTEL
Good afternoon, Fyedka.

                    FUEDKA
I came for the shirt.

                    MOTEL
It's ready.

                    TZEITEL
See, it's my new sewing machine.

                    FYEDKA
I see. I see. Congratulations.

                    MOTEL
Thank you.

                                    FYEDKA
                    (After another awkward moment)
Good day.
                    (Exits)

                                    MOTEL
Good day.

                                    GOLDE
How does it work?

                                    MOTEL
See, it's an amazing thing, you work it with your foot and
your hand.

                    (CHAVA exits from shop and meets
                    FYEDKA outside)

                                    CHAVA
I will, but I'm afraid.

                                    FYEDKA
Chava, let me talk to your father.

                                    CHAVA
No, that would be the worst thing, I'm sure of it.

                                    FYEDKA
Let me try.

                                    CHAVA
No, I'll talk to him. I promise ...

                    (TEVYE enters)

                                    FYEDKA
                    (Extending hand)
Good afternoon.

                                    TEVYE
                    (Takes hand limply)
Good afternoon.

                                    FYEDKA
                    (Looks at CHAVA)
Good day.
                    (Exits)

                                    TEVYE
Good day. What were you and he talking about?

                                    CHAVA
Nothing, we were just talking. Papa, Fyedka and I have
known each other for a long time now and ...

                                    89

                              TEVYE
Chava, I would be much happier if you would remain friends
from a distance. You must not forget who you are and who
that man is.

                              CHAVA
He has a name, Papa.

                              TEVYE
Of course. All creatures on earth have a name.

                              CHAVA
Fyedka is not a creature, Papa. Fyedka is a man.

                              TEVYE
Who says that he isn't? It's just that he is a different
kind of man. As the good book says, "Each shall seek his
own kind." Which, translated, means, a bird may love a
fish, but where would they build a home together?
                    (HE starts toward the Tailor Shop,
                    but CHAVA grabs his arm)

                              CHAVA
The world is changing, Papa.

                              TEVYE
No. Some things do not change for us. Some things will
never change.

                              CHAVA
We don't feel that way.

                              TEVYE
We?

                              CHAVA
Fyedka and I ... We want to be married.

                              TEVYE
Are you out of your mind? Don't you know what this means,
marrying outside of the faith?

                              CHAVA
But, Papa ...

                              TEVYE
No, Chava -- I said no! Never talk about this again! Never
mention his name again, never see him again. Never! Do you
understand me?

                              CHAVA
Yes, Papa. I understand you.

(GOLDE exits from the shop, followed
by SHPRINTZE and BIELKE)

GOLDE

You're finally here? Let's go home, it's time for supper.

TEVYE

I want to see Motel's new machine.

GOLDE

You'll see it some other time, it's late.

TEVYE

Quiet, woman, before I get angry. And when I get angry,
even flies don't dare to fly.

GOLDE

I'm very frightened of you. After we finish supper, I'll
faint ... Come home.

TEVYE
(Sternly)
Golde. I am the man in the family. I am the head of the
house. I want to see Motel's new machine, now!
(Strides to the door of the shop,
opens it, looks in, closes door,
turns to GOLDE)
Now, let's go home!

(THEY exit. CHAVA remains looking
after them on dimout)

DIMOUT

ACT II

Scene 6

                    TEVYE
          (Sinks down on cart)
How long can that miserable horse of mine complain about
his leg?
          (Looks up)
Dear God, if I can walk on two legs, why can't he on three?
... I know I'm very upset about my horse. He is one of
your creatures and he has the same rights I have: the
right to be sick, the right to be hungry, the right to
work like a horse ... And, Dear God, I'm sick and tired of
pulling this cart. I know, I know, I should push it awhile.

          (GOLDE enters, upset)

                    GOLDE
          (Offstage)
Tevye ...
          (Enters)
Tevye ...

                    TEVYE
          (Struck by her manner)
What? What is it?

                    GOLDE
It's Chava. She left home this morning. With Fyedka.

                    TEVYE
What?

                    GOLDE
I looked all over for her. I even went to the priest. He
told me ... they-were married.

                    TEVYE
Married!

          (SHE nods)

Go home, Golde. We have other children at home. Go home,
Golde. You have work to do. I have work to do.

                    GOLDE
But, Chava ...

                    TEVYE
Chava is dead to us! We will forget her. Go home.

          (GOLDE exits. TEVYE sings)

TEVYE

(Sings)
LITTLE BIRD, LITTLE CHAVALEH
I DON'T UNDERSTAND WHAT'S HAPPENING TODAY
EVERYTHING IS ALL A BLUR
ALL I CAN SEE IS A HAPPY CHILD
THE SWEET LITTLE BIRD YOU WERE
CHAVALEH, CHAVALEH.

LITTLE BIRD, LITTLE CHAVALEH
YOU WERE ALWAYS SUCH A PRETTY LITTLE THING
EVERYBODY'S FAV'RITE CHILD
GENTLE AND KIND AND AFFECTIONATE
WHAT A SWEET LITTLE BIRD YOU WERE
CHAVALEH, CHAVALEH

(CHAVA enters)

CHAVA

Papa ... I want to talk with you. ... Papa, stop. ... At
least listen to me ... Papa, I beg you to accept us.

TEVYE

Accept them? How can I accept them? Can I deny everything
I believe in? On the other hand, can I deny my own child?
... On the other hand, how can I turn my back on my faith,
my people? If I try to bend that far, I will break ... On
the other hand ... there is no other hand. No, Chava.
No -- no -- no ...

CHAVA

Papa ... Papa ...

PEOPLE   (CHORUS)
(Unseen, are heard singing as
CHAVA exits slowly)
TRADITION. TRADITION. TRADITION.

DIMOUT

93

ACT II

Scene 7

> The Barn. YENTE enters L, with
> two BOYS, teenage Yeshiva students,
> obviously uncomfortable in the
> situation.

YENTE

Golde, are you home? I've got the two boys, the boys I
told you about.

> (GOLDE enters, followed by SHPRINTZE
> and BIELKE)

Golde darling, here they are, wonderful boys, both learned
boys, Golde, from good families, each of them a prize, a
jewel, you couldn't do better for your girls ... just right.
From the top of the tree.

GOLDE

I don't know, Yente. My girls are still so young ...

YENTE
(Indicating BOYS)
So what do they look like, grandfathers? Meanwhile they'll
be engaged, nothing to worry about later, no looking
around, their future all signed and sealed.

GOLDE

Which one for which one?

YENTE

What's the difference, take your pick.

> (LAZAR WOLF, AVRAM, MENDEL, INN-
> KEEPER and OTHERS enter)

AVRAM

Golde, is Reb Tevye home?

GOLDE

Yes, but he's in the house. Why, is there some trouble?

AVRAM
(To GIRLS)
Call your father.

> (THEY exit)

                         YENTE
          (To BOYS)
Go home, tell your parents I'll talk to them.

          (THEY exit)

                         GOLDE
What is it? Why are you all gathered together like a bunch
of goats? What's ...

          (TEVYE enters)

                         AVRAM
Reb Tevye, have you seen the constable today?

                         TEVYE
No, why?

                         LAZAR
There are some rumors in town. We thought because you knew
him so well, maybe he told you what is true and what is not.

                         TEVYE
What rumors?

                         AVRAM
Someone from Zolodin told me that there was an edict issued
in Petrograd that all ... Shh. Shh.
          (HE stops as the CONSTABLE enters,
          with TWO MEN)

                         TEVYE
Welcome, your honor. What's the good news in the world?

                         CONSTABLE
I see you have company.

                         TEVYE
They are my friends.

                         CONSTABLE
It's just as well. What I have to say is for their ears
also. Tevye, how much time do you need to sell your house
and all your household goods?

          (There is a gasp from the OTHERS.
          THEY are stunned. THEY look to
          TEVYE)

                         TEVYE
Why should I sell my house? Is it in anybody's way?

                         CONSTABLE
I came here to tell you that you are going to have to leave
Anatevka.

                           95

                    TEVYE
And how did I come to deserve such an honor?

                    CONSTABLE
Not just you, of course, but all of you ... at first I
thought you might be spared, Tevye, because of your
daughter Chava who married ...

                    TEVYE
My daughter is dead!

                    CONSTABLE
I understand. At any rate, it affects all of you -- you
have to leave.

                    TEVYE
But this corner of the world has always been our home. Why
should we leave?

                    CONSTABLE
          (Irritated)
I don't know why. There's trouble in the world, trouble-
makers.

                    TEVYE
          (Ironically)
Like us!

                    CONSTABLE
You aren't the only ones. Your people must leave all the
villages -- Zolodin, Rabalevka. -- The whole district must
be emptied.

          (Ad libs from ALL)

I have an order here, and it says that you must sell your
homes and be out of here in three days.

                    ALL
Three days ... out in three days ... etc.

                    TEVYE
And you who have known us all your life, you'd carry out
this order?

                    CONSTABLE
I have nothing to do with it, don't you understand?

                    TEVYE
We understand.

                    MAN (THOM)
And what if we refuse to go?

                      96

                    CONSTABLE
You will be forced out.

                    LAZAR
We will defend ourselves.

                    OTHERS
Stay in our homes ... refuse to leave ... keep our land.

                MAN (MITCH)
Fight!

                    CONSTABLE
Against our army? ... I wouldn't advise it!

                    TEVYE
I have some advice for you. Get off my land!

          (ALL crowd toward CONSTABLE and
          HIS MEN)

This is still my home, my land. Get off my land!

          (MEN and CONSTABLE start off,
          CONSTABLE turns)

                    CONSTABLE
You have three days!

                MAN (THOM)
After a lifetime, a piece of paper and get thee out.

                    INNKEEPER
We should get together with the people of Zolodin. Maybe
they have a plan.

                MAN (THOM)
We should defend ourselves. An eye for an eye, a tooth for
a tooth.

                    TEVYE
Very good. And that way, the whole world will be blind and
toothless.

                    MENDEL
Rabbi, we've been waiting for the Messiah all our lives.
Wouldn't this be a good time for him to come?

                    RABBI
We'll have to wait for him someplace else. Meanwhile, let's
start packing.

                    MEN (MAURICE, SAM)
          (Starting to leave)
He's right ... I'll see you before I go ...

                    MAN (THOM)
Three days!

                    INNKEEPER
I have more than a hundred bottles of vodka. What will I
do with them?

                    MAN (TONY)
Where can I go with a wife, her parents and three children?

          (ALL are off except PRINCIPALS)

                    YENTE
Well, Anatevka hasn't been exactly the Garden of Eden.

                    AVRAM
That's true.

                    GOLDE
After all, what've we got here?
          (Sings)
    A LITTLE BIT OF THIS
    A LITTLE BIT OF THAT

                    YENTE
    A POT

                    LAZAR
    A PAN

                    MENDEL
    A BROOM

                    AVRAM
    A HAT.

                    TEVYE
Someone should have set a match to this place long ago.

                    MENDEL
    A BENCH

                    AVRAM
    A TREE

                    GOLDE
    SO WHAT'S A STOVE?

                    LAZAR
    OR A HOUSE

                         98

MENDEL

People who pass through Anatevka don't even know they've
been here.

GOLDE

A STICK OF WOOD

YENTE

A PIECE OF CLOTH.

ALL

WHAT DO WE LEAVE
NOTHING MUCH
ONLY ANATEVKA.

ANATEVKA, ANATEVKA
UNDERFED, OVERWORKED ANATEVKA
WHERE ELSE COULD SABBATH BE SO SWEET

ANATEVKA, ANATEVKA
INTIMATE, OBSTINATE ANATEVKA
WHERE I KNOW EVERYONE I MEET

SOON I'LL BE A STRANGER IN A STRANGE NEW PLACE
SEARCHING FOR AN OLD FAMILIAR FACE
FROM ANATEVKA

I BELONG IN ANATEVKA
TUMBLEDOWN, WORKADAY ANATEVKA
DEAR LITTLE VILLAGE, LITTLE TOWN OF MINE

GOLDE

Eh ... it's just a place.

MENDEL

Our forefathers have been forced out of many, many places
at a moment's notice ...

TEVYE

Maybe that's why we always wear our hats ...

DIMOUT

99

ACT II

Scene 8

                          Outside TEVYE's house. MOTEL and
                          TZEITEL are packing. SHPRINTZE
                          and BIELKE enter with bundles.

                     SHPRINTZE
Where will we live in America?

                     MOTEL
With Uncle Abram, but he doesn't know it yet.

                     SHPRINTZE
I wish you and the baby were coming with us.

                     TZEITEL
We'll be staying in Warsaw until we have enough money to
join you.

                     GOLDE
               (Enters, with goblets)
Motel, be careful with these. My mother and father, may
they rest in peace, gave them to us on our wedding day.

                     TZEITEL
Come, children --
          (To GIRLS)
Help me pack the rest of the clothes.

          (THEY exit into house)

                     YENTE
Golde darling, I had to see you before I left because I have
such news for you. Golde darling, you remember I told you
yesterday I didn't know where to go, what to do with these
old bones? Now I know! You want to hear? I'll tell you.
Golde darling, all my life I've dreamed of going to one
place and now I'll walk, I'll crawl, I'll get there. Guess
where? You'll never guess ... Every year at Passover, what
do we say? Next year in Jerusalem, next year in the Holy
Land.

                     GOLDE
You're going to the Holy Land.

                     YENTE
You guessed! ... And you know why? In my sleep, my husband,
my Aaron, came to me and said: Yente, go to the Holy Land.
Usually, of course, I wouldn't listen to him because, good
as he was, too much brains he wasn't blessed with. But in

                              YENTE (Continued)
my sleep it's a sign. Right? So, somehow or other, I'll
get to the Holy Land. And you want to know what I'll do there?
I'm a matchmaker, no? I'll arrange marriages, yes? So I'm
going to the Holy Land to help our people increase and
multiply. It's my mission. So goodbye, Golde.

                              GOLDE
Goodbye, Yente. Be well and go in peace.

        (THEY embrace)

                              YENTE
Maybe next time, Golde, we will meet on happier occasions.
Meanwhile, we suffer, we suffer, we suffer in silence!
Right? Of course, right.
                    (SHE exits. GOLDE sits on a large
                    straw trunk, sadly wrapping a pair
                    of silver goblets. TEVYE enters,
                    carrying a bundle of books, puts
                    them on the wagon)

                              TEVYE
        (Enters)
We'll have to hurry, Golde.

        (SHE is looking at goblets)

Come, Golde, we have to leave soon.

                              GOLDE
Leave ... it sounds so easy.

                              TEVYE
        (Indicating goblets)
We'll all be together soon. Motel, Tzeitel and the baby,
they'll come too, you'll see. That Motel is a person.

                              GOLDE
And Hodel and Perchik? When will we ever see them?

                              TEVYE
Do they come visiting us from Siberia every Sabbath? You
know what she writes. He sits in prison, and she works,
and soon he will be set free and together they will turn
the world upside down. She couldn't be happier. And the
other children will be with us.

                              GOLDE
        (Quietly)
Not all.

                        TEVYE
            (Sharply)
All. Come, Golde, we have to get finished.

                        GOLDE
I still have to sweep the floor.

                        TEVYE
Sweep the floor?

                        GOLDE
I don't want to leave a dirty house.
            (SHE exits behind the house as
            LAZAR enters, carrying a large
            suitcase)

                        LAZAR
Well, Tevye, I'm on my way.

                        TEVYE
Where are you going?

                        LAZAR
Chicago. In America. My wife, Fruma-Sarah, may she rest
in peace, has a brother there.

                        TEVYE
That's nice.

                        LAZAR
I hate him, but a relative is a relative! ...
            (Embrace)
Goodbye, Tevye.
            (LAZAR exits. TEVYE enters the
            house, passing TZEITEL, who enters
            with a blanket and a small bundle)

                        TEVYE
Tzeitel, are they finished inside?

                        TZEITEL
Almost, Papa.
            (TZEITEL puts the blanket on MOTEL's
            wagon, crosses DL with bundle, kneels,
            and begins rummaging in it. CHAVA
            and FYEDKA enter. TZEITEL turns
            to enter the house, sees them)
Chava!

            (CHAVA runs to her, THEY embrace.
            TZEITEL looks toward house)

Papa will see you.

                              CHAVA
I want him to.   I want to say goodbye to him.

                              TZEITEL
He will not listen.

                              CHAVA
But at least he will hear.

                              TZEITEL
Maybe it would be better if I went inside and told Mama
that ...

          (GOLDE enters around R of house)

                              GOLDE
Chava!
               (SHE starts toward her as TEVYE
               enters from house. HE sees them,
               turns, re-enters house, returns
               with a length of rope. HE crosses
               down to tie up the straw trunk,
               his back to CHAVA and FYEDKA)

                              CHAVA
Papa, we came to say goodbye.

               (HE does not respond, continues
               working)

We are also leaving this place. We are going to Cracow.

                              FYEDKA
We cannot stay among people who can do such things to
others.

                              CHAVA
We wanted you to know that ... Goodbye, Papa, Mama.
               (SHE waits for an answer, gets
               none, turns to go)

                              FYEDKA
Yes, we are also moving. Some are driven away by edicts ...
others by silence ... Come, Chava.

                              TZEITEL
Goodbye, Chava, Fyedka.

                              TEVYE
               (To TZEITEL, prompting her, as HE
               crosses upstage to another box)
God be with you!

                              TZEITEL
God be with you!

                              CHAVA
We will write to you in America. If you like.

                              GOLDE
We will be staying with Uncle Abram.

                              CHAVA
Yes, Mama.

          (THEY exit. TEVYE turns, watches
          them leave. There is a moment of
          silence; then HE turns on GOLDE)

                              TEVYE
We will be staying with Uncle Abram. We will be staying
with Uncle Abram. The whole world has to know our business.

                              GOLDE
Stop yelling and finish packing. We have a train to catch.

          (MOTEL, SHPRINTZE, BIELKE enter from
          the house)

                              TEVYE
I don't need your advice, Golde. Tzeitel, don't forget the
baby. We have to catch a train, and a boat. Bielke,
Shprintze, put the bundles on the wagon ...
          (TEVYE moves the wagon down center
          and MOTEL puts the trunk on it.
          Then THEY turn to one another for
          goodbyes)

                              TZEITEL
Goodbye, Papa.

                              GOLDE
Goodbye, Motel.

                              MOTEL
Goodbye, Mama.

                              TEVYE
Work hard, Motel. Come to us soon.

                              MOTEL
I will, Reb Tevye. I'll work hard.

          (TEVYE takes one last look at the
          baby, has a bit of babytalk, then
          TZEITEL and MOTEL exit with their
          cart. When THEY are gone, TEVYE
          turns to the wagon)

                    TEVYE
Come, children. Golde, we can leave these pots.

                    GOLDE
No, we can't.

                    TEVYE
All right, we'll take them.
          (Slams them down)

                    BIELKE
          (Childishly, swinging around with
          SHPRINTZE)
We're going on a train and a boat.

                    GOLDE
          (Sharply)
Stop that! Behave yourself! We're not in America yet!

                    TEVYE
Come, children -- Let's go.
          (TEVYE begins pulling the wagon
          against the turning revolve.
          OTHERS, including the FIDDLER,
          join in the circle. The revolve
          stops. There is a last moment
          together, and the OTHERS exit, at
          different times and in opposite
          directions. TEVYE begins to pull
          his wagon upstage, revealing the
          FIDDLER, playing his theme. TEVYE
          stops, turns, beckons to him.
          FIDDLER tucks his violin under his
          arm and follows the group upstage
          as ...)

               THE CURTAIN FALLS

FIDDLER ON THE ROOF

PERCHIK, THE STUDENT:

No.	Title	Page
1	"Prologue - Tradition"	1
14	"Sunrise Sunset"	32
22	"Now I Have Everything"	34

LAZAR WOLF, THE BUTCHER:

No.	Title	Page
6	"To Life"	16
31	"Anatevka"	42

MORDCHA, THE INNKEEPER:

No.	Title	Page
31	"Anatevka"	42

RABBI:

No.	Title	Page
11	"The Dream"	24
31	"Anatevka"	42

MENDEL:

No.	Title	Page
25	"The Rumor"	39
31	"Anatevka"	42

AVRAHM, THE BOOKSELLER:

No.	Title	Page
25	"The Rumor"	39
31	"Anatevka"	42

NACHUM, THE BEGGAR:

No.	Title	Page
31	"Anatevka"	42

GRANDMA TZEITEL:

No.	Title	Page
11	"The Dream:	24
31	"Anatevka"	42

FRUMA SARAH:

No.	Title	Page
11	"The Dream"	27
31	"Anatevka"	42

THE VILLAGERS: (CHORUS)

No.	Title	Page
1	"Prologue - Tradition"	1
4	"If I Were A Rich Man"	15
6	"To Life"	17
11	"The Dream"	25
14	"Sunrise Sunset"	31
15	"Wedding Dance - No.1"	33
25	"The Rumor"	38
30	"Chava Sequence"	41
31	"Anatevka"	42

No. 1   Prologue – Tradition

Moderato (in 2)

fade

Dai dai dai dai, Dai dai dai dai, Dai dai dai dai dai.

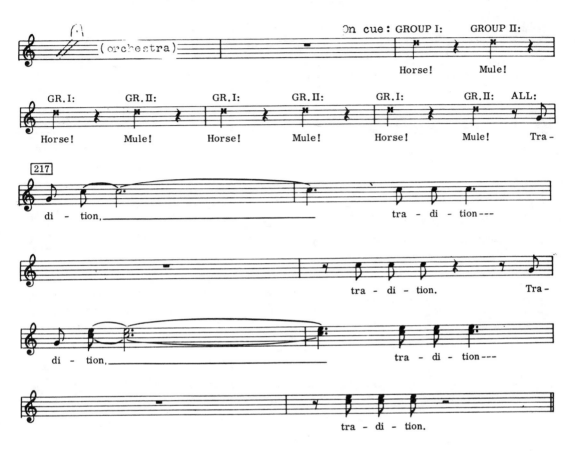

(orchestra)

On cue: GROUP I: GROUP II:

Horse! Mule!

GR. I: GR. II: GR. I: GR. II: GR. I: GR. II: ALL:

Horse! Mule! Horse! Mule! Horse! Mule! Tra -

217

di - tion, tra - di - tion---

tra - di - tion. Tra -

di - tion, tra - di - tion---

tra - di - tion.

No. 3   Matchmaker

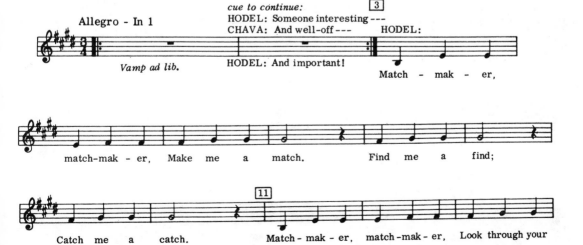

cue: TZEITEL: Oh, Yente --- Yente ---

Allegro - In 1

cue to continue: **3**
HODEL: Someone interesting ---
CHAVA: And well-off ---   HODEL:

Vamp ad lib.   HODEL: And important!

Match - mak - er,

match-mak - er, Make me a match. Find me a find;

Catch me a catch.

11   Match - mak - er, match-mak - er, Look through your

6

catch. Night af - ter night in the dark I'm a -

lone, So find me a match of my

own. _____

87
'n cue: TZEITEL:
(orchestra)
Ho - del, oh

Ho - del, Have I made a match for you! He's

hand - some! He's young! All right, he's six - ty two. But he's a

95
(spoken:)
nice man, a good catch --- true? True! I

prom - ise you'll be hap - py And e - ven if you're not, There's

103
more to life than that --- Don't ask me what!

109
(TZEITEL:)
Cha - va, I

found him! Will you be a luck - y bride! He's hand - some! He's

min - ute I mis - un - der - stood That I could get

160
CHAVA & HODEL:

stuck for good!_____ Dear Yen - te,

See that he's gen - tle. Re - mem - ber, You were

168

al - so a bride. It's not --- that ---

ALL THREE:

I'm sen - ti - men - tal, It's just that I'm

ter - ri - fied! _____

178 *marcato*

Match - mak - er, match - mak - er, Plan me no plans.

I'm in no rush. May - be I've learned:

186 Quietly

Play - ing with match - es a girl can get burned. So

190
Tempo I⁰

Bring me no ring. Groom me no groom.

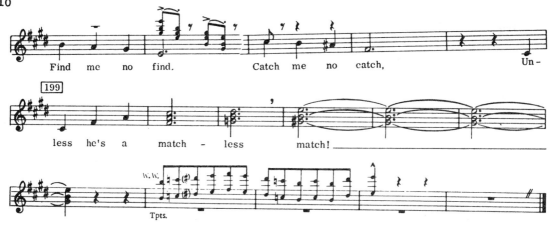

Find me no find. Catch me no catch, Un-

less he's a match - less match! _____

No. 4   If I Were A Rich Man

town. A fine tin roof with real wood-en floors be - low.

[28] There would be one long stair - case just go - ing up And

one e - ven long-er com-ing down. And one more lead - ing

no - where, just for show. I'd fill my yard with chicks and **[36]**

tur - keys and geese And ducks for the town to see and hear;

Squawk - ing just as nois - i - ly as they can.

[44] *(imitate animals —————————)* And each loud quack and cluck and gob - ble and honk Will

land like a trum-pet on the ear. As if to say: here

lives a wealth - y man._____ (Sigh)

[52] If I were a rich man, Dai-dle, dee-dle, dai-dle, Dig-guh, dig-guh, dee-dle, dai-dle

dum, All day long I'd bid - dy, bid-dy bum --- If I were a wealth-y

[60] man. Would-n't have to work hard, Dai - dle, dee - dle, dai - dle,

Sabbath Prayer

No. 6

To Life

OTHERS:
Za cha, za cha, za cha, za cha,

To your health and may we live to-geth-er in peace.

za cha, za cha, za cha, Hey!

189 Allegro - in 2
4 RUSSIANS:
(+ Vlns.)
May you both be fa-vored with the fu-ture of your choice.

May you live to see a thou-sand rea-sons to re-joice.

197
SOLO:
Vlns.
Ah_____ Ah_____

OTHERS: Fl., Cl.
Za va sha zda-ro-via. Heav-en bless you both, naz-dro-via.

Ah_____ etc. Ah_____ Hey!

To your health and may we live to-geth-er in peace._____ Hey!

No. 9 Tevye's Monologue

cue: MOTEL: We gave each other our pledge that we would marry.

One lit-tle time you pull out a prop And where does it stop? Where does it stop?

spoken:

Where does it stop?

44 Slowly - thoughtfully

They gave each oth-er a pledge. Un-heard of --- ab-surd! They

gave each oth-er a pledge. Un-think-a-ble! But look at my daugh-ter's face. She

51

loves him. She wants him. And look at my daugh-ter's eyes --- So hope-ful.__

No. 10   Miracle Of Miracles

cue: TZEITEL: Motel, you were wonderful.
MOTEL: It was a miracle.

Allegro, quasi agitato

It was a miracle.   *(hand claps)*

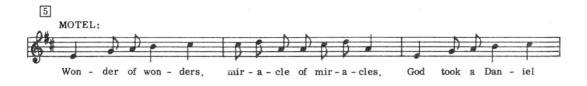

5 MOTEL:

Won - der of won - ders, mir - a - cle of mir - a - cles, God took a Dan - iel

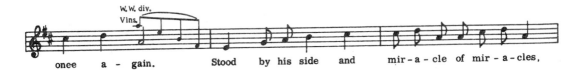

onee a - gain. Stood by his side and mir - a - cle of mir - a - cles,

Led him to the prom-ised land. When Da-vid slew Go-li-ath, Yes! That was a mir-a-cle.

Fl., Ob., Vlns.

When God gave us man-na in the wil-der-ness, That was a mir-a-cle, too.

But of all God's mir-a-cles, large and small, The most mi-rac-u-lous one of all Is the one I thought could nev-er be:

Rubato

Tempo

God has giv-en you to me!

No. 11   The Dream

Moderately - in 4

GRANDMA:

A bless-ing on your head,

RABBI: Ma-zel-tov, ma-zel-tov.

GRANDMA: To see a daugh-ter wed,

RABBI: Ma-zel-tov, ma-zel-tov.

GRANDMA:
And such a son-in-law Like no-one ev-er saw, The tai-lor, Mo-tel Kam-

GOLDE: GRANDMA: RABBI:
zoil. Mo-tel? A wor-thy boy is he, Ma-zel-tov, ma-zel-tov.

GRANDMA: RABBI: GRANDMA:
Of pi-ous fam-i-ly, Ma-zel-tov, ma-zel-tov. They named him af-ter my

Teyve
___ dear un-cle Mor-de-cai, The tai-lor, Mo-tel Kam-zoil. You must have

19 Più mosso
heard wrong, Grand-ma, There's no tai-lor. You mean a

GRANDMA:
(flies in rage)
butch-er, Grand-ma, By the name of La-zar Wolfe. No!

26
I mean a tai-lor, Tev-ye. My___

___ great-grand-child,__ My lit-tle Tzei-tel, who you

named for me, Mo-tel's bride was meant to be.

35 CHORUS: Ma-zel-tov, ma-zel-tov.
For such a match I prayed._____ In heav-en it was made.__

T+S

28

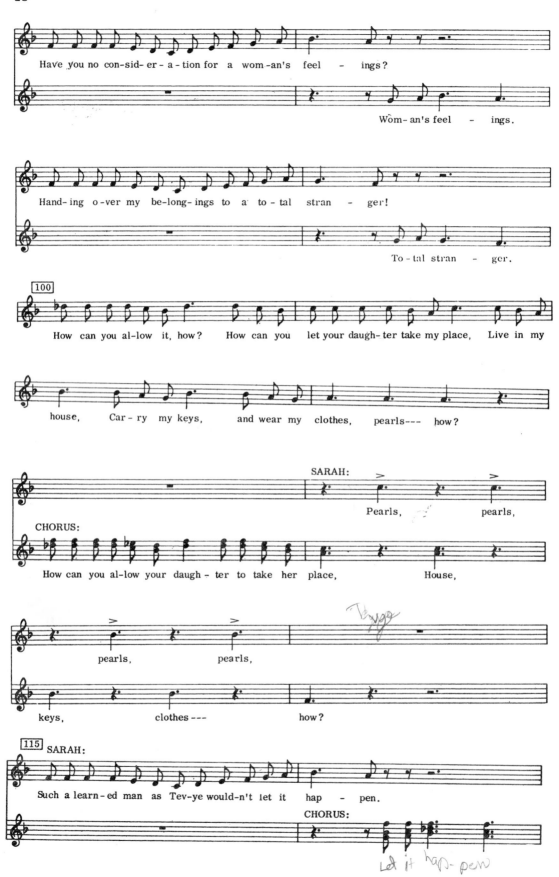

34

No. 21 Opening – Act II CHORUS TACET

No. 22 Now I Have Everything

cue: PERCHICK: I'm very happy, Hodel, very happy.

Moderate 4

HODEL: So am I, Perchick.
(on repeat) What's the matter?

PERCHICK:

I used to tell my-self That I had ev-'ry-thing; But that was on-ly half true. I had an aim in life And that was ev-'ry-thing; But now I e-ven have you. I have some-thing that I would die for— Some-one that I can live for, too. Yes, now I have ev-'ry-thing— Not on-ly ev-'ry-thing— I have a lit-tle bit more. Be-sides hav-ing ev-'ry-thing, I know what ev-'ry-thing's for.

I used to won-der Could there be a wife To share such a dif-fi-cult wan-d'ring kind of life?

HODEL: I was on-ly out of sight, wait-ing right here.

(Picc., Ob. 8va)

Tpt. I

Who knows to-mor-row

(HODEL:) I'll be with you and that's home e-nough for me.

Where our home will be?

Ev-'ry-thing is

right at hand--- BOTH: Sim - ple and clear.___

39 Più mosso Fl., Cls. (Octaves)

PERCHIK:

I have some-thing that I would die for;

Some-one that I can live for too. Yes, Now I have ev-'ry-thing---

Quasi march
+Vlns., Vla.

Not on-ly ev-'ry-thing--- I have a lit-tle bit more. Be -

Tpts.

47 Rubato [Embrace]

sides hav-ing ev-'ry-thing, I know what ev-'ry-thing's for.___

No. 23   Tevye's Rebuttal

TEVYE: You're not asking for my permission?

HODEL: But we would like your blessing, papa.

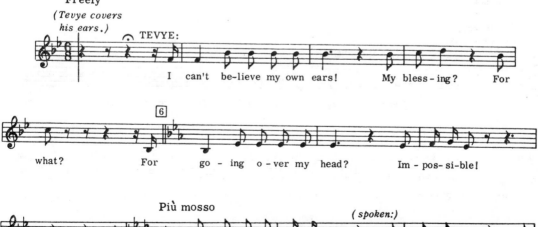

Freely

(Tevye covers his ears.) TEVYE:

I can't be-lieve my own ears! My bless-ing? For

6

what? For go - ing o - ver my head? Im - pos- si-ble!

Più mosso   *(spoken:)*

At least with Tzei-tel and Mo-tel, They asked me--- They

No. 24   Do You Love Me?

twen-ty-five years I've lived with him, **Fought** with him, starved with him,

twen-ty-five years my bed is his. If that's not love, what is? Then you love me? I sup-pose I

TEVYE: GOLDE:

TEVYE:

do. And I sup-pose I love you too.

BOTH:

It does-n't change a thing, But e-ven

so, Af-ter twen-ty-five years It's nice to know.____

No. 25 The Rumor

On Cue:

(YENTE:) Rifka---Rifka, I have such news for you!

(YENTE:)

Re - mem-ber

Per-chik, That cra - zy stu - dent? Re - mem-ber at the wed-ding, When

In 4

Tzei-tel mar-ried Mo-tel And Per-chik start-ed danc-ing with Tev-ye's daugh-ter Ho-del? Well,

OTHERS: YENTE:

I just learned that Per-chik's been ar - rest-ed in Ki - ev. No! Yes!

Ist WOMAN: Shaindel, Shaindel! Wait till I tell you!

(Ist WOMAN:)

Re-mem-ber Per-chik, that cra-zy stu-dent? Re-mem-ber at the wed-ding? He

danced with Tev-ye's Ho-del. Well, I just heard that Ho-del's been ar - rest-ed in Ki-ev.

No. 26 Far From The Home I Love

No. 30
Chava Sequence

No. 31

Anatevka

cue: YENTE: Well - - -

After all ... etc.

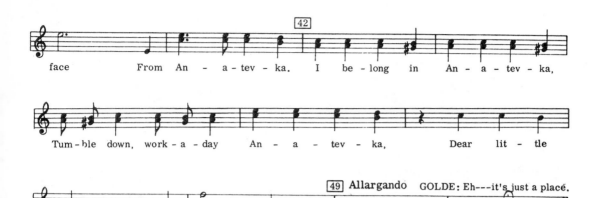

face   From An - a - tev - ka.   I   be - long   in   An - a - tev - ka,

Tum - ble down, work - a - day   An - a - tev - ka,   Dear   lit - tle

[49] **Allargando**   GOLDE: Eh---it's just a placé.

vil - lage, lit - tle   town   of   *ten.* mine.